THE GOOD ENTREPRENEUR

Copyright © 2022 Nick Kennedy
All rights reserved. No part of this publication may be reproduced, distributed, or transmitted in any form or by any means, including photocopying, recording, or other electronic or mechanical methods, without the prior written permission of the publisher, except in the case of brief quotations embodied in critical reviews and certain other noncommercial uses permitted by copyright law. For permission requests, write to the publisher, addressed "Attention: Permissions Coordinator," at the address below.

hello@sleepinggiantbooks.com

ISBN: 979-8-9851376-0-6 (print)

Sleeping Giant

ISBN: 979-8-9851376-1-3 (ebook)

Ordering Information:
Special discounts are available on quantity purchases by corporations, associations, and others. For details, contact hello@sleepinggiantbooks.com.

Scripture taken from THE MESSAGE. Copyright © 1993, 1994, 1995, 1996, 2000, 2001, 2002. Used by permission of NavPress Publishing Group.

NICK KENNEDY

THE GOOD ENTREPRENEUR

An Insider's Guide to Building a ~~Perfect~~ Principled Business and a Powerful Personal Legacy

TABLE OF CONTENTS

Introduction 1

Principle One 7
Choose Courage Over Fear

Principle Two 19
Fight for Purpose Not for Power

Principle Three 33
Seek and Tell the Truth

Principle Four 45
Leverage Desperation to Find Inspiration

Principle Five 55
Make Intentional Decisions

Principle Six 69
Ask for Help

Principle Seven 85
Live Your Values, Even When No One Is Looking

Principle Eight 101
Eschew the Good for the Best

Principle Nine 117
Stay Scrappy to Survive

Principle Ten 129
Optimize in Any Situation

Principle Eleven 143
Thrive in Business and Life

Principle Twelve 163
Leave a Powerful Personal Legacy

Endnotes 183

Acknowledgments 191

INTRODUCTION

Entrepreneur.

Who do you think of when you hear that word?

Steve Jobs
Oprah Winfrey
Jay-Z
Elon Musk
Sara Blakely
Richard Branson
Wendy Kopp
Henry Ford
Jeff Bezos
Herb Kelleher
Arianna Huffington
Thomas Edison
Sam Walton
Howard Schultz

What do all these people have in common?

They've all made a positive impact on our world and, most likely, your life.

Steve Jobs put a supercomputer in millions of pockets. Sara Blakely created Spanx, a company dedicated to helping women have more confidence. Howard Schultz put a great cup of coffee on over 32,000 corners across the globe.[1] Wendy Kopp put thousands of teachers in classrooms in underdeveloped areas with her organization Teach for All.[2] Jeff Bezos made countless items available in 17 countries.[3] Oprah Winfrey created a worldwide community from inside our television sets.

It's incredible how much one individual can change society. These entrepreneurs built businesses that they believed would propel humanity to the next level. They created innovations they had faith would make the future better. They faced criticism and skepticism that could have shut them down completely.

So often, people can't see the dream until an entrepreneur makes it reality. Why? Because that's what entrepreneurs do. Entrepreneurs make fiction into reality.

And the world needs that. The world needs entrepreneurs.

For too long, we've reserved the term *entrepreneur* for the small subset of the population that is running startup companies or is part of accelerator programs or on the cutting edge of the latest breakthrough technology. They are the entrepreneurs. They are the innovators. They are the changemakers.

But what about the rest of us? Spending our weekends working on a dream we don't know if we'll ever realize? Leading a team of people toward a goal in the office? Driving forward to build a small business? Attending classes at college, knowing most of what you are learning will never be used after graduation? Hoping to escape the world given to you by creating a new path for you and your family? Do we really share the same essence as Steve Jobs? As Elon Musk? As Oprah Winfrey?

Are we *really* entrepreneurs?

I am writing this book because *I believe entrepreneurship can be learned.* I believe you *can* be an entrepreneur. We *need* you to be. I hope this book will help you see that in yourself and provide a map for your entrepreneurial journey.

I've been an entrepreneur for most of my adult life. It started with a pancake-making business in my dorm room and has, most recently, led to me launching, growing, and selling an airline. There were many ventures in between, and along the way, I've interacted with, observed, and worked alongside other entrepreneurs of all backgrounds. I've compared our personal experiences, our distinct characteristics, and our unique paths to the places we ended up.

The world measures our successes by the end results—the products we create, the businesses we build, the status we achieve. Although those are incredibly important keys to measuring the success and stamina of an entrepreneur, they offer a narrow view of who these men and women—these entrepreneurs I've encountered along the way—really are. It's a view that's missing the spirit of entrepreneurship altogether, the spirit that I think is in *all* of us.

Entrepreneur is a French word that means "to undertake," as in to undertake a business venture. The Irish French economist Richard Cantillon further defined the term as a person "making decisions about obtaining and using the resources while consequently admitting the risk of enterprise."[4] Both these definitions give an accurate description and a more inclusive understanding of what it is to be an entrepreneur. They acknowledge the willingness of the entrepreneur to *assume a risk* and *deal with the uncertainty* that follows. My definition of an entrepreneur is "the bearer of risk."

Who among us can't relate to that?

If the definition of an entrepreneur is someone who bears risk, then the term can be more broadly defined. Now we can begin to see ourselves in the mix.

Home builders are entrepreneurs.
Chefs are entrepreneurs.
Artists are entrepreneurs.
Engineers are entrepreneurs.
Physicians are entrepreneurs.
Pastors are entrepreneurs.
Plumbers are entrepreneurs.

Architects are entrepreneurs.
Stay-at-home parents are entrepreneurs.
Consultants are entrepreneurs.
Coaches are entrepreneurs.

If you're the chief executive officer (CEO) of an organization, not only are you likely an entrepreneur, but your employees are entrepreneurs as well. You might not have considered that before, but you want them to think of themselves that way. You want them to be able and willing to *assume a risk* and *deal with the uncertainty* that follows. **Uncertainty is where growth comes from.**

Whether you are the head of the latest tech unicorn, the sous-chef at a thriving restaurant with dreams of starting your own, the founder of the hottest electric car company, or a roofer employing three people and finding a way to make payroll each month, you're an entrepreneur.

Entrepreneurs have an incredible capacity to create positive change in the world. And with a little bit of willingness to be the bearer of risk, you get to join our ranks.

Risks are everywhere. The uncertainty is palpable. And because of that, we're all invited to play the entrepreneur's game.

Hear this: if you bear risk, you are an entrepreneur.

But in the midst of this ever-changing world we're living in, I believe that bearing the risk is worth the reward. In fact, entrepreneurship may be more important today than it ever has been, given the issues humanity is currently facing. We cannot afford to exclude ourselves from the narrative simply because we don't want to take on risk. Entrepreneurs will forever be at the center of innovation and change. They always have been. *And the world needs you, the entrepreneur willing to take the risk, to make it possible.*

Am I asking you to quit your job and start chasing that dream immediately? Not necessarily. What I'm saying is that this is a path—and this is a book—for anyone looking for more purpose in their position. It's for the CEO running a successful business and the single parent trying to make ends meet. It's for the corporate leader close to retirement and the brand-new hire just starting out.

For anyone who wants their work to have meaning and create a positive impact in the world, I believe entrepreneurship is the vehicle that gives them the greatest chance to do so.

And it all starts by embracing a new way.

The way of not just an entrepreneur, but the way of the Good Entrepreneur.

Good Entrepreneurs have a moral obligation to change the world for the better by following these 12 principles.

> Principle #1. The Good Entrepreneur chooses courage over fear.
> Principle #2. The Good Entrepreneur fights for purpose, not for power.
> Principle #3. The Good Entrepreneur seeks and tells the truth.
> Principle #4. The Good Entrepreneur leverages desperation to find inspiration.
> Principle #5. The Good Entrepreneur makes intentional decisions.
> Principle #6. The Good Entrepreneur asks for help.
> Principle #7. The Good Entrepreneur lives their values, even when no one is looking.
> Principle #8. The Good Entrepreneur eschews the good for the best.
> Principle #9. The Good Entrepreneur stays scrappy to survive.
> Principle #10. The Good Entrepreneur optimizes in any situation.
> Principle #11. The Good Entrepreneur thrives in business and life.
> Principle #12. The Good Entrepreneur leaves a powerful personal legacy.

By learning the way of the Good Entrepreneur, we will not only help our companies and corporations sustain the risky and constantly evolving nature of our times, but we will also gain something so much more valuable in the process: positive change for ourselves and our communities.

The journey to become a Good Entrepreneur is not for the faint of the heart, but this book is my invitation to you to take a risk to become something bigger than yourself.

The world needs more Good Entrepreneurs, and this book is written to help you see that you—yes, you—can be just that.

PRINCIPLE ONE

CHOOSE COURAGE OVER FEAR

A STARTING PLACE

I have an ongoing debate with my friend Trey Bowles about whether people are born with the entrepreneurial instinct or if anyone can be taught the way of the entrepreneur. We have discussed this question with our fellow entrepreneurial friends, and their answers vary based on their personal experiences. Certain personality traits certainly lend themselves to helping on the entrepreneurial journey, but there are plenty of stories about people who used entrepreneurship as a way of survival, learning the necessary skills along the way. But regardless of where they eventually land on this question, all entrepreneurs acknowledge that *no one* will become an entrepreneur without one very specific trait: the courage to start the journey.

After the airline I cofounded was acquired, I decided to change my vocation from building businesses to supporting the people who are building businesses. Now, I have the privilege of working alongside entrepreneurs as an advisor, helping them connect their personal and professional lives on the longest journey in the world—the 18 inches between their hearts and their minds. In doing so, I get to hear their stories and influence their journeys. They come from every kind of socioeconomic or educational background, race, religion, and sexual orientation. They are a living testament that there isn't a one-size-fits-all description of an entrepreneur.

This is not to say that they all start equally, in fact, quite the contrary. Everyone's starting line is placed according to their birth lottery. Some end up placed a few meters ahead of the official start line, some a few meters behind, and some outside the stadium with one hand tied behind their back, missing a shoe.

I started out my life ahead of many others, born as a White man in the United States. However, I wasn't fully aware of that privilege until my father was sentenced to 20 years in prison when I was 16. Suddenly, my upper-middle-class life was ruptured irrevocably. I was moved toward the back of the pack. I didn't have a clue how to operate in this new, less privileged position. But I had to learn—fast.

Talk about bearing risk. Not only did I have to learn how to survive, but I also needed to learn a whole new way of operating if I was ever going to accomplish my dreams. I didn't know it at the time, but entrepreneurship was the bridge that would allow me to cross the chasm between the world that had been handed to me and the world I wanted, although the journey would be even more treacherous than I had imagined.

I am writing this book because I want to help you make that excursion yourself—to cross the chasm between the world you've been handed and the one you dream about. Wherever you're starting from and whatever you bring to the table, I want to remind you that you are equipped to make a positive impact on this world.

But in order to do it, you'll need to see yourself as an entrepreneur. And not just any entrepreneur but a Good Entrepreneur. *I've learned firsthand that entrepreneurship is not a sprint or a marathon; it is more like an Ironman Triathlon.*

The journey gives plenty of time for those whose lot in life left them behind the starting line to catch up, and it only yields to those who refuse to quit. The starting point may differ, but the process levels the playing field. It gives everyone the chance to tear down society's norms, lay waste to the powers that be, and leave a dent in the universe.

But only those of us who can tap into the courage to start will find out how the race is run.

THE ENTREPRENEURIAL JOURNEY

Let me let you in on a secret: Good Entrepreneurs choose courage over fear. It's what sets them apart—because this entrepreneurial journey is not for the faint of heart.

Picture yourself at the start of this road. It often begins with frustration and, more frequently, desperation. From the very beginning, you are required to make risky decisions, and the first is to decide between two choices: give in to fear or get going. Courage helps you do the latter. And since desperation is often the mother of invention, a solution arises. A gadget, a service, a piece of software, or maybe a whole new category of industry is dreamed up.

The entrepreneur inside of you begins to emerge.

Then, courage carries you forward. You share the idea with your close friends (but only the ones that won't make fun of you too much!).

"Why hasn't anyone thought of this?" you ask them. "It would make our lives so much easier."

They agree and encourage you to take the next step. To find out what it would take to keep going and keep growing and to turn this fiction into reality.

That momentum carries you so swiftly that you begin to be led by it, and before you know it, you are dreaming up names, buying URLs, and wondering how your Wikipedia entry will read once the world recognizes your genius. You begin mentally burning your metaphorical boats, quitting your job, cashing out your 401(k), asking friends and family for money, and declaring with confidence that you've finally found what will give you purpose in this world.

Then, you launch. You put your heart's work out into the world. And suddenly, momentum isn't as easy to come by. You find yourself falling ever so quickly into what I call the *trough of despair*, wondering why you ever quit your safe, okay-paying job and your overbearing boss. Your inner critic starts to whisper in your ear:

> You were never cut out for this.
> Why were you such a fool, cashing out your entire 401(k)?
> Did you really think you could make this work?
> Can you eat rice and beans for the rest of your life?

You consider turning back, but it's too late for that. You are halfway down the path now. This is where the rubber meets the road. It's here on the entrepreneurial journey that we are truly tested, but it's through this testing that we get to see what we are really made of.

You could begin the slow, uphill battle, manipulating yourself and others to move your business forward. And all for what? So that you can wake up tomorrow morning to fight another day?

Or you could choose another path. One that leans into the courage that motivated you in the first place. One that doesn't give in to quick fixes or desperate attempts. One that moves you toward meaning. If you can find the courage to start walking that path, then you're one step closer to becoming the Good Entrepreneur this world needs.

LOOKING BACK

Choosing courage over fear isn't a new concept in entrepreneurship. In fact, it's been the motivation for entrepreneurs for thousands of years. It's given them the power to solve the world's greatest problems, to shape the culture we're living in, and to irrevocably change the course of history forever. This may sound like hyperbole, but I assure you, it's not.

How do I know? Because we have thousands of years of evidence pointing to the entrepreneurial spirit as the catalyst for growth in humankind. In every business, corporation, or position, it's that courage—that entrepreneurial spirit—that first pushed them forward to progress.

Not convinced? Let's look at our past.

The first inventions crafted by humans were stone tools some two and half million years ago.[5] The second invention was fire, some 1.7 million years ago.[6] The third and arguably most important invention in the history of human development was entrepreneurship in the form of trading estuarine snail shells called Nassarius, some 80,000 years ago.[7]

The shells had human-made holes suggesting use as jewelry. "Either people went to sea and collected them, or more likely marine shell beads helped create and maintain exchange networks between coastal and inland peoples," says Francesco d'Errico,[8] lead author and director of research at the French National Centre for Scientific Research (CNRS). But these shells tell a story well beyond ornamental use. Scientists believe that the shells represent a technology used to communicate through a coded language. This advancement in humankind indicates advanced intelligence and the development of behaviors that might link to the spread of humans out of Africa.

Keep in mind that at that point in human history, *Homo sapiens* (Latin: "wise man"[9]) and Neanderthals shared the Earth. In fact, one of the theories regarding the extinction of Neanderthals is violent conflict over limited resources.[10] Contrast that with *Homo sapiens* who established a division of labor through the *bearing of risk* (entrepreneurship), allowing isolated tribes to benefit from the resulting efficiency. By learning to trade, humans divided labor in an exchange that allowed both parties to walk away better off because of it. A tiny snail ushered in a new way of thinking, one that would forever change the trajectory of humankind.

That was entrepreneurship at its genesis.

Fast-forward to around 6,000 BC when our Egyptian ancestors settled in the Nile delta. Bearing the risk of moving to a new land had been worth it for these settlers, for the flood plains they migrated to contained the perfect agricultural ingredients of water and nutrient-rich soil to grow crops plentifully. In addition, they found security. With the technology of transport limited to what you could carry yourself, it was impossible for a hostile force (whether a predator or warring tribe) to approach without being detected.[11]

For one of the first times in the history of humans, we weren't spending the majority of our time seeking shelter and food. This combination of food surplus and security also gave way to a surplus of labor. We were able to spend time on pursuits other than simply surviving. Attention could be focused on things like irrigation canals, building an army, and creating additional inventions, from metallurgy to writing.

Are you seeing how entrepreneurship—the solving of problems through taking calculated risk—allowed humans to evolve and progress?

Over the next several thousand years, societies leveraged excess labor to build pyramids, create and maintain the Alexandrian library (with the equivalent of one hundred thousand books), and replace wood and stone tools with copper.[12]

Around 2,000 BC, cities started to appear around the world, concentrated mainly around rivers such as the Nile, Tigris, Euphrates, Indus, Yellow, and Yangtze. Trade routes were established between these cities, and some became large, with up to fifty thousand people in cities like Uruk and Sumeria (modern-day Iraq). Individual skilled labor was still the primary means of entrepreneurship, but a new class of entrepreneurs was trading coffee, lemons, and oranges from Arabia to Europe, salt from Africa across the Roman Empire, and sharing complex ideas like the Arabic number system, brought to Europe by Leonardo Fibonacci.[13] (See, even math teachers can be entrepreneurs!)

Prior to this point in history, we don't know most of the names of the entrepreneurs. Instead, we think of them as a conglomeration of individuals whose courageous first steps moved humanity forward. However, in 1712, progress accelerated in ways no one could have imagined.

Thomas Savery, an engineer from England, conceived the steam engine, and in doing so, he helped in creating the first ever hockey-stick growth in terms of human development (picture a graph in the shape of a hockey stick—this is the turning point where growth starts and when there's no turning back). The first steam engine was used to pump water out of coal mines, allowing them to dig deeper and mine more coal. It was the first self-powering technology. The more powerful the steam engine, the more coal it could produce, and that in turn lowered the cost of the coal used to power it.[14]

Unlike wind and water, coal was a solid object that was used for power, smelting, and transport far from the location where it was mined. By 1800, the technology had matured enough that steel became available in high volumes. Steam engines became smaller and powerful enough to move steamships and locomotives, lowering the cost and increasing the speed of delivery of goods at a rate that had never been seen before.[15]

Savery couldn't have possibly understood the implications of his invention at the time, but he changed the course of history with it. This entrepreneur became the catalyst for the fastest increase in humanity's quality of life that the world had ever seen.

Luke Muehlhauser, a researcher who studies risks to human civilization, created the following graph by comparing six different metrics for human wellbeing.[16] The six metrics he charted were life expectancy; gross domestic product (GDP) per capita; the percentage of the population living in extreme poverty; "war-making capacity," a measure of technological advancement for which we have the most historical data; "energy capture," which reflects access to food, livestock, firewood, and, in the modern day, electricity; and the percentage of people living in a democracy.

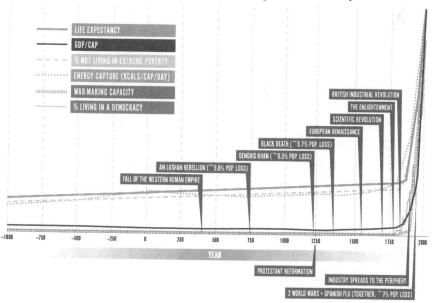

Can you imagine that 1,700 years after Jesus walked the Earth, there had not been much measurable progress for all of humanity?

Savery's step of courage changed all that. It jump-started the engine of progress. Fast-forward another 150 years, and entrepreneurs like Andrew Carnegie, J. P. Morgan, John D. Rockefeller, and Henry Ford leveraged these powerful forces to continue to move society forward. They might not have even used the word *entrepreneur*, but they used their talents and gifts to take calculated risks for the good of all. With the benefit of hindsight, we can look back at this very short period (1700–1900) and marvel at the power of entrepreneurship. The steam engine kicked off the Industrial Revolution and, in turn, changed the course of humanity.

What could be possible if *you* bore a risk as they did?

WHAT'S AT STAKE?

This type of advancement has been increasing at a rapid rate ever since the Industrial Revolution. Take a minute and think of the implications of this. In 1970—only 50 years ago—there was no internet, no space shuttle, no MRI, no Prozac. Only twenty years ago, there was no iPhone, no GPS, no digital camera, no Tesla, and no Instagram. Because of entrepreneurs, a journey from London to Wales, which in 1800 would have cost a month's wages, is 50 times faster today and one-thirtieth of the cost. In the 1950s, it took 30 minutes of work to earn the price of a McDonald's cheeseburger; today it takes three minutes. Besides health care and education, few things cost more now than they did 50 years ago (at least in terms of hours worked).[17]

Looking back at 1920, most luxuries of that day would be described as "below the poverty line" by today's standards. Today in America's designated "poor areas," 99 percent have electricity, running water, flushing toilets, and a refrigerator. Even J. P. Morgan, for most of his life, could not have said the same. This growth is not just limited to America. All throughout Europe, Africa, and Asia, electricity, refrigerators, and running water can be seen in even some of the most rural villages.[18]

Entrepreneurs, whether in the form of business owners, scientists, artists, engineers, inventors, or teachers, have given us clean water, higher literacy rates, new technology, and medical advancements.

At the turn of the century in 2000, compared to just 50 years earlier, quality of life had increased significantly in terms of money earned, calories consumed, and life expectancy. As Matt Ridley documents in *The Rational Optimist: How Prosperity Evolves*, humans were "less likely to die as a result of war, murder, childbirth, accidents, tornadoes, flooding, famine, whooping cough, tuberculosis, malaria, diphtheria, typhus, typhoid, measles, smallpox, scurvy or polio." Literacy had increased, education had flourished, and technology had become prevalent whether in the form of telephones, toilets, or refrigeration.

And that is all in the last few generations! The rate of progress and development by any standard is an astonishing achievement. And it's that progress that's at stake for future generations if the entrepreneurs of today—people like you and me—don't find the courage to start.

The watch manufacturer Patek Philippe has one of the greatest marketing taglines in the world: "You never actually own a Patek Philippe. You merely look after it for the next generation."[19]

Entrepreneurs also never really own entrepreneurship: they merely look after it for the next generation. As a father of three children, my role is to help them become a better version of themselves while I become a better version of myself. As a Good Entrepreneur, my role is to help the next generation be more successful than my own.

All the innovation we enjoy today? The progress we live through? The communities we have? They came about because someone was willing to have the courage to be the bearer of risk. Our responsibility is to honor the risk they took by acknowledging the shoulders that we are standing on.

The power of entrepreneurship has not only been harnessed by these people that we know so well; it has also been harnessed by millions of other people you have never heard of. Some of these people have been quietly running successful businesses for decades. I've met, advised, talked to, and interacted with thousands of entrepreneurs all over the map, and I can tell you with confidence that *all* of them experienced the transformative process of entrepreneurship. They were changed. They had the courage to bear the risk, and they received the reward of the journey.

KEEP STARTING

After the airline I cofounded was acquired, I forced myself to take several years off before starting a new venture so that I could reflect on my own journey. Through hard work and the help of several kind and intentional souls, I was able to remove many of my blind spots and see the truth of my situation. During my journey, I thought I was holding the weight of the world on my shoulders, and it was slowly crushing me. As C. S. Lewis said, "Prosperity knits a man to the world. He feels that he is finding his place in it, while really it is finding its place in him."[20]

I had let the entrepreneurial journey and the accompanying prosperity become my identity, and it nearly ended my marriage, a handful of relationships, and any hope of leaving a lasting legacy. Why am I confessing this to you? Because I want to make sure the same doesn't happen to you. Or if it does, you're able to come out on the other side stronger for it at the very least.

In order to be the Good Entrepreneur the world needs, we have to focus on where we begin. Again and again and again, we'll find ourselves starting over along the way. Over and over and over, we'll have to dig deep to find the courage to keep starting. The Good Entrepreneur doesn't just find their courage at the start of their journey; they find it every step of the way. And they let it be the momentum that carries them forward.

If you are in the middle of your journey and the road has twisted unexpectedly, you might feel lost and ready to abandon your journey. *I see you.* I have been where you are. I've stood where you're standing. Most of us are walking in the dark, arms outstretched, just hoping not to fall off a cliff. We all need courage in those moments.

If you are writing the obituary of your failed venture, I salute you. It took tremendous courage to start, continue, and finally shut the door on your dream. Know that Walt Disney was fired from one of his jobs because he "lacked imagination and had no good ideas."[21] And Oprah Winfrey was fired from one of her first TV jobs because she was "unfit for television."[22]

Your courage to start proves you have what it takes to start again.

Or if you have finished the first major part of your journey and you're trying to make sense of everything that's happened so far, know that I see you too. Remembering your own journey and reflecting on the decisions you've made along the way takes courage in that moment too.

Every Good Entrepreneur longs to live a life of meaning, to leave a legacy that makes the world better.

And every Good Entrepreneur's road begins with the courage to start.

END-OF-CHAPTER HOMEWORK
REAL VS. IDEAL LIFE

So, what do we do? If we want to be Good Entrepreneurs, where do we find the courage to start? Well, the first thing we need to do is take account of where we are.

Take out your journal or find a blank piece of paper and draw a horizontal line. To the left of the horizontal line, write "Real" and on the other end write "Ideal."

Now, consider where you are right now in your life on that line. The *ideal self* is the person who you would like to be; the *real self* is the person you actually are.

Be honest! Although most of us long for the ideal—plenty of money, time to meditate, a happy spouse and kids, supportive friends, a benevolent inner judge, openness, creativity and love—the truth is we all tend to be living further from the ideal than we'd like.

So many of us aren't anywhere near where we want to be in our lives. We're living in the gap between real self and ideal self, and this is causing an incongruent life. We experience congruence when our real self and ideal self are closely related. High congruence leads to a greater sense of self-worth and a healthy, productive life. Now, make a mark on the line where

REAL ──────────────→ IDEAL

you are *right now* on the journey from ideal to reality. We now have the starting place so we can know where we are working from.

If your line is not near the "Ideal" side of the line, this is the moment where you have to choose courage over fear. We could deny there's a gap in our lives between where we are and where we want to be. We could attempt to rely on sheer willpower to close that gap. We could judge ourselves critically for our perceived failures or fall into despair that we can't make the ideal real.

Or we could find the courage to get real. To simply start. To keep starting as many times as it takes.

If you have never walked this journey before, I am going to ask you to trust me on this one. At this point in the journey, you can't script what is going to happen. You can't force an outcome. You can't manipulate your way to your ideal life. You have no choice but courage here. And the Good Entrepreneur chooses courage, not just for their own sake but for the sake of others.

This is the moment in the entrepreneurial journey in which the gift of entrepreneurship begins to reveal itself to you. Because courage doesn't come easy, and that means you'll need help to find it. So, if you're struggling to find the courage to start, ask someone to come alongside you as you go.

If the line you created is close to the ideal, congratulations! You have become what many wish to become. Now your job is to continue to find ways to grow, stretching yourself to places you've never gone. As you do, you also need to find ways for helping others on their journey. The framework in this book can be used as a filter for helping you determine how best to do so.

PRINCIPLE TWO

FIGHT FOR PURPOSE NOT FOR POWER

PRIVATE PLANES

I got a call from my friend James a few years ago.

"You're a Denver Broncos fan, right?" he asked immediately, not even answering my hello. "There is a Broncos player who wants to meet you and have dinner with you. You free anytime soon?"

I have a rule about taking meetings on the spot like that. I say no, unless there's a reason for the meeting that's compelling enough to carve out the time. It's a cardinal rule of mine, and I *never* break it. But the moral of this story is that you should never say never, because I said yes to this meeting without even thinking. I guess a dinner date with a future Hall of Fame football player, who also happened to play for my beloved Denver Broncos, was my deal breaker.

Within a few days, I was on my way to Denver in a private plane.

I had always dreamed of flying on private planes. I would look at them from a distance as I schlepped through the commercial terminal at airports, wondering what the insides looked like, smelled like, and felt like. Now that I had arrived, I knew exactly what it felt like. And though it was not quite beyond my wildest dreams, it was exactly what I wanted.

"We should have clear sailing from here on out," the pilot said, breaking my train of thought. "I'll let you know if that changes."

I nodded back at him and smiled.

A private plane is better than the second house or the third supercar; it's the ultimate decadence because of the freedom it provides.

Sometimes, when you know that pilot well, they let you sit in the right seat, the one beside them in the cockpit. You put on the headphones and listen to the chatter of the skies between the various pilots and air traffic controllers. Scanning the instrument panel full of gauges and maps might be confusing at first glance, but the captain will often patiently answer all of your questions. He might even allow you to take control of the yoke and move the plane from side to side, ever so gently, as if you're holding a brand-new baby in your arms.

Having flown hundreds of hours in private planes, I can tell you that the real benefit of flying private comes in the currency of time. A private plane is magical because it is a time machine.

Instead of going to the major airport, you choose the one that happens to be closest to your house. Instead of going to the parking garage and hoping that you find a space, you pull up to the security gate, push the button on the intercom, announce your name and the tail number of the plane you are flying on, and watch the gate open while you drive through.

Instead of waiting in line at security, taking off your shoes, and removing all liquids over 3.4 ounces from your bag, you pop your trunk, and an attendant comes around to usher your bags onto the plane. The pilots, in their crisp white shirts, open your door and shake your hand to welcome you.

Instead of rushing through the airport and searching for a coffee line without 25 people in it, the flight attendant hands you your almond-milk cappuccino and helps you settle in with that day's copy of *The New York Times* and *The Wall Street Journal*.

Instead of watching 160 other passengers board the plane, bump your shoulder as they make their way down the aisle to their seat, and fight over the last remaining baggage spot, the captain informs you that there was a report of a little bit of chop north of Amarillo, so they are going to increase the elevation to a little higher and a little further south. The good news? That should hopefully give you a great view of Palo Duro Canyon, the second largest canyon in the United States, on this beautiful summer morning.

And instead of fighting for your bag in the overhead compartment and being bum-rushed by other passengers headed for the exit door when you land, you are handed your sport coat, freshened up by the flight attendant, and wished a great day.

"We'll be waiting for you when you get back. Good luck in your meeting," the crew says.

Stepping outside and onto the tarmac at this small airport, you spot the driver of the car that was reserved for you and hand him your bag.

"What brings you to town, Mr. Kennedy?" the driver will ask as you settle into the back of his new BMW 7 series.

A SYMBOL OF POWER

There is no greater symbol of power than the private plane. Every time I stepped aboard one, I truly felt untouchable. I thought I had done it. I thought had crossed the chasm and had made it. And each flight seemed to be proof of that.

After arriving in Denver on this particular trip, I entered the dining room and saw the man whom I had seen play football on TV so many times. He was smaller than I had imagined. His jewelry, however, was as impressive as I thought it might be, signaling the contract he had just signed. The small talk was anything but usual as we discussed the ups and downs of playing in the NFL, particularly in Denver.

Apparently the "downside" was that the nightlife left something to be desired for NFL players, so one of his teammates had built a club in the basement of his house where the team would go to blow off steam. The upside, as I learned that night, was that the altitude of 5,280 feet above sea level had a way of exhausting and demoralizing visiting teams, particularly in the fourth quarter.

"Do you ever trash-talk to the other team?" I asked, laughing at his impression of the other teams practically limping up and down the field.

"We can hardly breathe either!" he chuckled.

I peppered him with questions, not staying nearly as cool as I would have liked but also not wanting to miss the opportunity to ask him what was on my mind.

We started with cocktails and then transitioned to Silver Oak wine when the steaks arrived. The restaurant wasn't busy on this Tuesday night, but our table was the center of attention.

Throughout our meal, my dinner companion kept referencing PJs. For a good hour, he would say things like "I remember my first time in a PJ. It was so cool," or "PJs are the best! You can leave a practice and be gone twenty minutes later."

I wondered why he wanted to talk about pajamas, the only reference to PJs that I was familiar with at the time. Finally, when a break came in the middle of the conversation and I had a little liquid courage in my blood stream, I spoke up.

"Excuse me, but why do you keep referencing pajamas? I am a little lost."

"Man, what are you talking about?" he responded.

"You keep referencing PJs. What are you referring to if not pajamas?" I said.

"You are hilarious!" he cackled to himself, practically falling off his chair. I laughed a little too, feeling only slightly self-conscious.

"I am talking about private jets!" More cackling.

He looked like he was convulsing, he was laughing so hard. And just when I thought the laughter might slow down, it picked right back up again.

He was right about one thing. The PJ industry had a completely different prestige than any other industry I had been involved in. And if I'm being honest, I liked it. It was the status symbol recognized around the world.

If you were rich, if you were famous, if you had really and truly made it, then the private plane showed it. It showed your power.

As dinner wrapped up, my new friend offered to let me use his suite at the stadium whenever I wanted, and I secured tickets to the Tom Brady vs. Peyton Manning game that was coming up in a few months. We said our goodbyes, and in the back of the car on the way to the airport, I texted the pilot that we would be there in 15 minutes. He replied to let me know they'd be ready—"wheels up" as they say—five minutes after we arrived. I was whisked through the security gates and onto the plane, settling into the same seat I had occupied hours earlier, barely sitting down before I was handed an Angel's Envy rye Manhattan for the flight home. I opened my phone and fired up my hot tub so that it would be the perfect temperature when I arrived home an hour and half later. Looking into the dark sky, it dawned on me that the business we had created—an airline of private planes—was something that even professional athletes were impressed with and wanted to be associated with.

What made our airline unique was that we didn't have passengers; we had members—passengers suggest a transaction, whereas members create a relationship. And those members paid a monthly subscription fee for unlimited scheduled flights that they got to share with other members, actual people you wanted to talk to on a flight because they were the movers and shakers of the community. And all of these flights happened on private airplanes, the kind you see celebrities flying on. And because we used those planes, we also used private terminals. It was a game-changing experience for our members, the majority of whom had never been in a private plane and because the plane was shared, the cost was much more affordable than flying by yourself.

Even for a dreamer like me, conceiving and launching an airline was reaching beyond even my wildest fantasies, yet as I sat in my seat on my way home, I felt like I had arrived. I had power, or at least I thought I did. And deep down, isn't that what every entrepreneur is seeking when they start?

Or is it something deeper than that?

I think this quest for power felt all the more real to me because of where I'd been before I ever sat inside the plush seat of a private plane. I'd seen what I thought was the opposite of power and prestige, and I didn't want to find myself there again.

PRISON VISITING ROOMS

"Make sure you take out all of your change, keys, and metal objects from your pockets and put them through the metal detectors."

As I stepped through the metal detectors, the high-pitched alarm went off.

"I told you to empty your pockets," chastised the authority figure on the other side.

From the sound of his voice, the prison guard wanted to be in prison about as much as I did. Yet here we both were, him doing his job and me visiting my father.

The year before this visit, I had turned 16, and I was the first in line to take my driver's test on a chilly morning in San Diego. In one final act of normalcy, my father drove me to the Department of Motor Vehicles and signed me in for the test. An hour later, I walked out of the office with my license and a new lease on life. I did not know it then, but my childhood had effectively ended. I was about to face a life disruption of epic proportions.

Within a few months, my father would go on trial in Colorado, be convicted of several white-collar crimes, and be sentenced to 20 years in federal prison. This process took the better part of my 16th year on this Earth, but it felt like it happened in a matter of seconds.

Sometimes life is too much to handle, and ignoring all the signs or stuffing them deep down inside is the easiest reaction in the moment. *Human resilience is one of the most powerful tools we have, but it costs us dearly until we force ourselves to take a full account of its effects on us.* Much to my detriment, it took me several decades to do so.

This particular visit to my father was one of the first times I had seen him in prison. I wasn't there with my family; I was with my friend Mark. Earlier that year, Mark had moved to Illinois from San Diego to live with his father. When that plan didn't work out and he decided to move back to California, I begged my parents to let me drive with him, promising I'd stop in Denver to see my dad on the way.

I still don't know why they agreed to allow two 16-year-old kids to drive 2,000 miles across the United States, but trauma does that to you. It makes you numb to reality.

When we arrived at the prison, I went inside while Mark waited in the truck. Having completed the forms and passed through the metal detector, I waited for my dad to enter the visiting room. When he did, he looked like a shell of the man who was once my hero. His fake smile did not conceal the consternation of his mind. His skin was pale, his hair disheveled, and he wore an ill-fitting prison jumper and black shoes.

There is nothing to prepare a child for seeing their parent in prison. It was like receiving a swift kick to the stomach. I couldn't speak. I hurt in a place somewhere deep inside myself. We hugged, and I was comforted by the fact that his musk was still familiar. But that was all I recognized. The lion that was my father had been replaced by an injured lamb.

Looking back, I can't imagine the trauma my father was experiencing. He protected me from all the stories of what life was really like in there. There were things I wanted to know but was afraid to ask. Was it like the stuff TV dramas were made of? Or was it worse? I decided I could live without knowing the truth.

The conversation meandered awkwardly during that visit. We were like two strangers forced to talk to one another. We filled the space with sentences that began without knowing how they would end. We relied on small talk to take up our time.

If a private plane is the symbol of power, this was the exact opposite. Freedom was restricted, luxury constrained, and respect nonexistent. The only thought you think in the prison visiting room is how to end that nightmare.

I didn't know it at the time, but my affinity for private planes was born in that prison waiting room. What I really wanted, as I sat there talking with my dad, was freedom. I wanted the freedom to go where I wanted, when I wanted without constraint, both literally and metaphorically.

A PRISON OF OUR OWN MAKING

There's no doubt that, at the age of 40, I'd attained the success I had dreamed of and then some. The airline we started? We named it RISE. It was meant to be a play on the analogy of the plane taking off, but it also represented what we were helping our members do in their lives.

Rise.

Rise above their circumstances. Rise to the level of success they dreamed of. Rise to the occasion. Rise to power.

That's what most entrepreneurs are after, right? Money, success, or power? PJs? Even if that isn't the goal at the start of this journey, it certainly becomes one along the way. And let me just stop and say this: none of those things are bad! Gaining wealth, growing in power, looking for more success? Those are all well and good! The problem comes when those become your identity because then we lose sight of what's real.

It's so easy to confuse symbols of power with real power. Planes, cars, hot tubs, and dinners with NFL superstars are symbols. They're illusions we chase in the pursuit of power. I was blinded by these illusions—these mirages seducing me at every turn.

But can I let you in on a little secret? Something I think every Good Entrepreneur should know?

Those outward symbols of power can become *prisons of our own making*.

All of it can come with a cost. Having access to a private plane outwardly means that you've made it, but what is happening on the inside? What have you gone through mentally, physically, and emotionally to get there? And what do you have to keep going through in order to stay there? You may have "made it," but you'll most likely never be able to stop sprinting on the internal treadmill that never turns off.

I have known many people with access to countless symbols of power, but many of these people (including myself) would tell you that although the private plane may look like freedom, we feel trapped. Stuck on a never-ending trek to gain more or to keep what we have. Surrounded by expectations at every turn, wondering who our real friends are and who only wants us for what we can give them. We are pushed forward on a quest for power that creates a prison of our own making.

REAL POWER

I don't want you to make the same poor decisions I did. I don't want you to be the kind of entrepreneur who confuses private planes for power. I want you to be the Good Entrepreneur—the kind who chooses *real* power.

And the good news for you? Real power is already at your fingertips. It's already within you. Maybe your circumstances make you believe otherwise. Maybe you're the lowest person in the pecking order in your office. Maybe you're broke and not sure how you're going to finance this dream. Maybe you're a CEO on the verge of a break. Maybe you're a kid visiting your dad in prison. Whoever you are, the truth is this: your circumstances don't determine your identity. I thought they did, but that belief almost led to the destruction of my life. As the Irish poet John O'Donohue reminds us, "Your identity is not equivalent to your biography."[23]

Your circumstances don't define you unless you let them. You already have everything within you that you need to turn your life from where it is now to somewhere completely different. You have real power right now. Real power comes from knowing what your purpose is.

Good Entrepreneurs don't ask *what should I do* but rather focus on the most important question, which is *how should I be?*

A PATH TO PURPOSE

Like most things in life, unlocking your purpose is easier said than done. The path to purpose isn't linear. It looks different for all of us. And it certainly isn't as glamorous as the path to symbolic power might look. But trust me when I tell you the path to purpose—the path of the Good Entrepreneur—will leave you with more freedom than any private plane will ever offer.

Purpose begins with understanding that *your life matters.*

Sitting in that prison waiting room, I had never felt so dark. Whatever hope I'd had left about what my life might hold for me was squeezed out of me with each minute that I stayed in that room. I was itching to get on the road and out of that nightmare. I rejoined my friend Mark as quickly as I could.

We decided to hit the road to Las Vegas on the way home, hoping to find some fun for a couple of 16-year-olds. As we left, the sun was starting to set. It was a cool, crisp fall day in Denver. The clouds were gathering in the mountains, sending a signal to not try to cross them this evening, but we ignored it.

Mark opened the cover on top of the truck bed and hopped in the back. He planned to get some sleep there while I navigated the terrain for the night. As I drove us up I-70 toward Vail, snow started to fall heavily from the sky. It was almost dark, and the effect of the snow through the windshield looked like the hyperspace scene from *Star Wars*; the stars seem to stretch until they disappeared.

Soon, our truck started to struggle to make it up the mountain. The tires were slipping and sliding up the slick four-lane road. It was getting dicey, carving through the canyons of the Rocky Mountains. Out of nowhere, I hit a piece of ice that sent the rear wheels of our truck spinning and sent the truck into a slow-motion circle. I lost control of the vehicle. Nothing I did with the steering wheel had any impact on where we went.

Eventually, the truck slammed into the middle divider of the freeway facing downhill, grating metal on concrete, sending sparks flying, and leaving us shaking from head to toe. From the bed of the truck, I could hear Mark cursing, trying to gain his bearings before everything went silent. The truck was now at rest in the fast lane facing downhill.

I turned the key, but the engine wouldn't turn over. Over and over again, I tried to start that truck but to no avail. That's when a flash of light caught my eye. It was an 18-wheeler, fully loaded, bearing down on us like a steam locomotive.

What if this truck hit the same piece of black ice, spun out of control, and hit our little truck?

Truth be told, the irony of our position wasn't lost on me. My dad was in prison, I felt lost, without purpose, and I had thought a few times about committing suicide, not believing I had anything worth living for now that my dad was where he was. Shame and embarrassment hung around my neck like an anchor. I wondered if, in fact, this was the mercy of God on me—to take me out on this snowy road with a quick explosion. Maybe this was how I would finally find the peace I had so desperately been looking for.

But the strangest thing happened to me in that moment. I realized that I didn't want to die.

As the truck approached the piece of black ice, now less than 50 feet from our position, it didn't seem to be slowing down the slightest bit. The truck driver pulled on his horn and lit up the mountains with a loud cacophony that echoed through the canyon. I closed my eyes, allowing my ears to be my only guide at this point. My hands were wrapped around the steering wheel, knuckles white under the strain, and my feet pushed full force into the brake pedal as if I could somehow will my way out of this situation.

When the truck came within 10 feet, I only had one thought going through my head. It appeared with such dramatic clarity that I *knew* it was important. I *knew* it was something I would remember forever.

The thought?

If I can get out of this situation alive, I *can* fix everything else in my life.

Just like that, clarity. And in that clarity, peace. And in that peace, purpose.

There was silence again. I opened my eyes to see the truck passing. We were still alive, still in our truck, still downhill in the middle of a snowstorm.

Today was not our day to say goodbye. Instead, it was a day to choose a new path.

There on the mountain in the middle of the road, my mindset had changed. I didn't want to die. I wanted to live.

And not just live but live with purpose. I wanted to make it home to San Diego. I wanted to go to college, get married, and have beautiful babies. I wanted to care. I wanted to live a life that wasn't determined by others' decisions. I wanted to be *more* than a victim.

I want that for you too (though I hope you find it without the near-death experience!).

So how do you find your purpose?

You start by deciding that your life matters. That you have a purpose. That you want to be here. That you want to contribute something of value. That the world needs what you can contribute to it. And you allow that sense of purpose to drive you forward no matter what happens. Even when it seems like everything is falling apart. Even when the worst happens. Even when your dad is in prison. Even when you're on the wrong side of a mountain road with a semitruck barreling toward you. Allow yourself to believe that *everything is fixable*.

I know what you're thinking.

That's too simple. You don't understand my situation.

I'm sure it sounds that way. But trust me, there's more in later chapters.

And in order to get there, we need to start with the end in mind. This next exercise is going to stir up rumblings inside of you that will begin to whisper your purpose.

END-OF-CHAPTER HOMEWORK
HOW DO YOU FIND PURPOSE?

Write your obituary. Although this might seem morbid at first blush, how can we know where we are going if we don't know where we want to end? It can be as long or as short as you want, but it should include at least three sections:

- What will people say about you when you aren't around?
- How did you go about creating this life that people speak about?
- The other part of your history that makes up who you are.

Don't worry about making this perfect. You are the only who is going see this (for now). Just get some thoughts down on paper. We will go into more detail later in the book about this, but for now, take time to reflect on the days you have on this Earth and what you will do with them.

I encourage you to look up the obituaries of people whom you respect. And as an example, I have included the obituary that I have created for myself:

NICK KENNEDY WAS A LOVING HUSBAND, devoted father, and a loyal friend. When he wasn't spending time loving on those he loved, he became the salt and light to many people through his entrepreneurship, writing, and coaching ventures. Nick was never afraid to hear the truth or to tell the truth, and most people left conversations with him changed for the better. He created experiences that led to truth telling and life change for billionaires, prisoners, and everyone in between.

His first book, *The Good Entrepreneur*, became a bestseller and stayed on the list for several decades, helping his readers cultivate lives that matter. He went on to write 10 more books, ranging from poetry to business books focused on connecting the physical, spiritual, and emotional life as one. Prior to his writing career, he was a successful entrepreneur, launching, running, and selling an airline, RISE, which was his "thing before the thing."

He was born in Fort Collins, Colorado, and was raised there and in San Diego, California, alongside his older brother, Robby, and older sister, April, by their parents Bill and Debbie Kennedy. He received a baseball scholarship to play baseball at Harding University where he met the love of his life, Angela (Sholl) Kennedy, the Grammy-winning artist. They lived in Dallas, Texas; Steamboat Springs, Colorado; and the British Virgin Islands, and had three children: Will, a world-renowned psychologist and inventor of the Smell Recorder, Sam, the lauded artist and chair of the Museum of Modern Art in NYC, and Jane, the first female president of the United States.

PRINCIPLE THREE

SEEK AND TELL THE TRUTH

TO TELL THE TRUTH

It seems really simple, right? *Seek the truth. Tell the truth.* Then why do we as humans have such a hard time doing it?

The memory of a strong rebuke or overstep from the past can hold fresh in our minds, making honesty feel like a relational risk. But as hard as it is to get real with each other, it can be even more difficult to be honest with ourselves—sometimes even impossible to tell the truth to ourselves.

Some of this comes from our lack of desire to truly *know* the truth. To know the truth, we'd have to explore outside of order and risk peeking into chaos. So instead, we spend our time and energy projecting our insecurities and issues onto other people, making them the problem while pretending like everything is just fine with us. (As a side note, and in my experience, *FINE* stands for F*cked Up, Insecure, Neurotic, and Emotionally Unstable.)

But what might be possible if we were willing to step into the chaos to find the truth? We might discover the purpose and meaning we've been longing for.

This is the way of the Good Entrepreneur.

CHAOS AND ORDER

I have a client who had portrayed that everything was working well in her life, but there were hints that told a different story. In one conversation, the carefully crafted facade came tumbling down.

"On the outside, I look like I have it all together. The home in the right neighborhood, the sports cars, a month of vacation in Spain, a handsome husband, and two bright kids. But the truth is I am completely bankrupt inside. I don't know who I really am. I'm constantly morphing depending on the situation I am in. During the daytime, I seem to be able to hold it together, but when I lay my head on the pillow at night, I toss and turn, worrying about the charade I am keeping up and wondering when I will be found out. I have friends I don't fully trust and a husband that barely speaks to me, not to mention a nonexistent sex life. I am afraid my son has learning disabilities, and I found a joint in my daughter's bedroom last week. To make matters worse, my business partners want to invest in a new product, and I have no available cash to put toward it. We're barely making our payments on our current obligations. I've dug myself deep into a hole like I always do—like my father said I would—and I don't know what I am going to do."

The other nine people in the group we were in sat quietly as the tears ran down her face. She began to sob, her truth spilling out with every tear.

The confessions of my client weren't shocking to me. From our first phone call, I could tell that she was barely holding it together. People are constantly telling things about themselves—sometimes they even use words. She was exhausted from keeping up appearances. Of course, initially she didn't acknowledge this verbally. But once I started really listening, I could hear the truth trying to break through.

But you can imagine why she wasn't *thrilled* about going there.

Chaos is the unexplored territory. It's the person who is different from you. It's the idea that doesn't match your ideology. It's the fear that your incompetence will be exposed or that the skeleton in the closet will one day walk out into the open. Chaos is the feeling when your best friend lies to you, or your spouse cheats on you, or your child is arrested. It is the dragon that cannot be slayed. When you live in chaos, your dreams fade. You don't know who you are, what you're doing, or why you're doing it.

Nobody loves to explore the chaos. We crave order.

But here's the problem. When you avoid chaos, you avoid opportunities for growth. Not only do your dreams fade, but so do the dreams of others. All innovation, invention, and possibilities start in the world of chaos. That's where truth can be found. And that's why we must risk going there.

Yes, truth—the kind of truth that sets you free—can be right smack dab in the middle of the chaos. And although most of us are just hoping we don't have to touch that chaos with a 10-foot pole, the Good Entrepreneur knows that if they're ever going to uncover the truth, they're going to have to venture into the unknown.

Don't get me wrong. There's nothing wrong with order. Order is a safe home to live in, a place with food on the table, and a family that trusts one another. It is faith in an entity, or a country, or a currency where everyone knows the value and hierarchy. It is the job that you have held for years. It's the one thing that is uniquely your own, providing two of your most basic human needs: security and identity. It is trusting that you're accepted despite your inadequacies because the other person knows they are the same. It is the feeling you have when you hold your newborn baby in your arms, and for a moment in time, they are perfect.

When your kids respect you, that's order. When they go to rehab, that's chaos. When you make a profit in your business, that's order. When your business partner embezzles money from you, that's chaos.

Most entrepreneurs crave order but thrive in chaos. The Good Entrepreneur thrives in the balance between the two.

CONSCIOUSNESS

In between order and chaos lives a third option. That option is consciousness, and that is where the Good Entrepreneur thrives.

Consciousness, as I'm using it here, is just a fancy way of saying *truth*. To say that I'm conscious means that I'm someone who seeks and tells the truth.

When Adam and Eve took a bite of the apple in the garden, they became *conscious*. They became aware that the paradise that they inhabited, while seemingly perfectly ordered, was bordered by a world of chaos. In other words, they saw the truth.

We know this balance between chaos and order because it is inherently built within us and the stories we have been telling since the beginning of time. It is found in the Bible: "God created the Heavens and Earth—all you see, all you don't see. Earth was a soup of nothingness, a bottomless emptiness, an inky blackness" (Genesis, 1:1–2, MSG). It's in the ancient Romans writings: "I found Rome a city of bricks and left it a city of marble."[24] It's even seen through Sebastian the crab in *The Little Mermaid*: "Listen to me. The human world, it's a mess."[25]

The reason that moment of confession in my client's life was so valuable was because she became conscious. She saw things as they were, and she was willing to tell the truth!

It's a beautiful intersection: chaos and order. This is where consciousness lives. This is the point of the yin-yang symbol, a perfect circle with the white side embodying order and the black side embodying chaos. But within the side of order, there is a black dot, hinting that order is not perfect, that a serpent can enter the garden. And within the side of chaos, there is a white dot, reminding us that even the most chaotic season can be redeemed. Both chaos and order touch each other, closer than is comfortable and necessary to be conscious and fully alive.

When we have an honest, objective view of ourselves and our lives, then and only then can we begin to have the impact we long for. Straddling these two worlds, fully conscious and openly honest, is the embodiment of being mature. It's the way of the Good Entrepreneur.

WHAT YOU NEED TO BE SUCCESSFUL

Over the course of my career, I've had countless conversations with leaders who hold incredible positions of wealth and power but still feel insecure about the positions they hold. There is a common refrain I hear whispered: "If you only knew the truth ..." In other words, "If you only knew what I really struggled with or what was truly going on with me, you'd see me very differently than you do." I even once heard the preacher Haddon Robinson say during a sermon, "If you knew me the way God knows me, you probably wouldn't like me."

The world tells us what we need to be successful: an Ivy League education, a ton of wealth, all the books and podcasts you can fill your time with, a subscription to the *Harvard Business Review*, and more strategies and tactics than the next person. But let me tell you—the one quality that will make you successful over and above any of those things is an ability *to seek and tell the truth*. If you can see a situation clearly, tell the truth about what you see, and admit to yourself and others that you don't have all the answers, that will be far more powerful than a diploma from a prestigious university.

Let me share three stories to show you what I mean.

A young man from New Jersey went to college but dropped out after his freshman year. He moved to New York City, raised some money, and launched a credit card company that gave "social perks" to its members. After that project faltered, he went into business with a rapper turned businessman, and they launched a product that gave people access to celebrities through their proprietary platform. They then decided to launch a music festival on a Caribbean island. The launch video went viral, thanks to the help of social media influencers sharing images of models frolicking on a beach, laughing, playing, and looking like they didn't have a care in the world. Almost eight thousand people bought tickets. This young man continued to raise money, borrowing nearly seven million dollars leading up to the event. Sound familiar yet? When the thousands of fans flew to the island for the festival, they didn't find supermodels sipping champagne at a luxury resort. Instead, they found FEMA tents, slimy sandwiches, and an equally slimy entrepreneur trying to control the unruly crowds with a bullhorn. Social media feeds were filled with the truth, and this entrepreneur could no longer spin his way out of trouble. He was eventually indicted, convicted of fraud, and sentenced to prison. This is the story of Billy McFarland[26] and the Fyre Festival.[27]

The next story is about a young woman who grew up in Texas and went to Stanford. She, too, dropped out of college after dreaming of a product that could forever change the medical field. Focused on the mundane but necessary world of blood testing, she invented a machine called the Edison that could apparently run dozens of tests using only a single drop of blood. Investors flocked to her idea, giving her company a valuation of 10 billion dollars and making her the world's youngest self-made female billionaire at the age of only 30. She, too, continued to raise money, each round of fundraising providing the necessary cash to stay alive. Walgreens signed on as one of the first clients and began to roll out the testing to the public. The only problem? The results they showed didn't come from the Edison but rather the older testing systems that had been around for decades. A book called *Bad Blood* was written by a *Wall Street Journal* reporter, and the whole fraud came crashing down.[28] As the company imploded, it negatively affected her 800 employees, two former U.S. secretaries of state, a former U.S. secretary of defense, two former U.S. senators, a former U.S. Navy admiral, a U.S. Marine Corps general, and two CEOs of publicly traded companies, the latter of whom were tasked with providing oversight on the board of directors in exchange for being richly rewarded in compensation. This is the story of Elizabeth Holmes, who fought to the bitter end and denied the reality of her situation.[29]

The final story is about two friends who were upset that they had to spend nearly eight hundred dollars to hire a private driver. To solve the problem, they decided to build an app that could hail cars on demand. Their company began to grow rapidly, starting in San Francisco and spreading quickly to New York, Paris, Singapore, Los Angeles, London, Boston, and other major cities all over the world. They used dubious and often illegal tactics for their meteoric rise, preferring to ask for forgiveness instead of permission. With nearly 110 million users worldwide, its popularity is undeniable, yet the company is fraught with issues. Harassment allegations, a frat-boy culture, and a win-at-any-cost mentality culminated in several scandals, including illegally obtaining the medical records of a rape victim in India. The CEO was finally fired, and the new CEO began to install a culture of truth telling. When they finally disclosed their financial numbers for their upcoming IPO, the public was stunned. They were generating billions in revenue, but they had yet to turn a profit, losing as much as five billion dollars in one quarter. This is the story of Travis Kalanick and his company Uber.[30]

Now, let's just imagine for a second that these three entrepreneurs—Billy, Elizabeth, and Travis—decided to get real. During the most trying times in their lives, imagine if they had chosen to be completely honest with themselves and each other.

"I am in way over my head," Travis would hopefully have said. "I promised the world transportation on demand that was as readily available as running water, and they believed me. If they only knew the shortcuts I took to get to this place."

"You think you have it bad? I promised to change medical care for everyone on the planet," Elizabeth might add. "I had an idea at the age of 19, and it took off from there. The intoxicating combination of the press and investors fueled our growth. But as it turned out, I lacked the maturity to look at the truth of the matter and realize that I didn't know what I had signed up for."

"At least you're not in prison," Billy would chime in. "It is hell in here. Knowing what I know now, I should have pulled the plug on the whole concert. At one point, I thought about doing just that. But I had lies piled on lies, so many that I couldn't see the truth. I knew that if I pulled the plug, I would get sued and potentially end up in prison anyway. So, I rolled the dice to see if I could pull it off."

"Did we have the option to stop the chaos that was consuming us?" they would ask.

"We had no choice but to see our stories through to the end, no matter what the circumstances," they might conclude. "We burned our ships at the shore, and there was only one way out: straight ahead."

"Yeah, and I'm the one who famously said, 'The minute you have a backup plan, you've admitted you're not going to succeed,'" Elizabeth remembered.[31]

And that is certainly one choice. But the Good Entrepreneur knows, in the depths of an honest moment, there is another way. It's truth that will help us find it.

A BETTER WAY

Sitting with leaders in their most vulnerable moments has taught me a lot. Primarily, it's taught me that the way of the Good Entrepreneur—the better way—is available to all of us. We just have to choose to be leaders who can be honest. Leaders who can be vulnerable. Leaders who can tell the truth.

Let me share three more stories to show you what I mean.

Over two decades ago, my friend bought a lawnmower and started mowing lawns. His ever-ready smile, Texas work ethic, and generous personality got him his first client and then several more. As his success became public, a jealous competitor sued him and almost stopped his progress completely. He fought with what little money he had and prevailed—barely. Morning after morning, he toiled away long before the sun came up and well into the hot Texas days. He hired an employee to help with the work and then several more to keep the company going and growing. Some months were better than others, but he stood ready for the challenges of the journey of the entrepreneur, choosing to make decisions that would benefit him in the long run rather than simply looking to make a quick buck.

The stress of running the business negatively affected both his health and his marriage. But instead of giving up and giving in, he chose a better way. He chose to work on his relationship, focus on the health of himself and others, and grow his business in a way that valued honesty. Ultimately, he found financial success. He now has multiple homes, drives any car he wants, and flies on a private plane frequently. But more than that, he has found relational success. People who know him well would say he is the most generous person they know, offering to pick up checks at meals, paying for trips, supporting nonprofit organizations, and leaving outlandish tips for servers when he hears of the hard times they are going through. His employees have had their lives changed for the better because of his genuine desire to see them build a better life for themselves. He could have chosen the path of least resistance, but instead, he chose a path of a Good Entrepreneur. This is the story of my friend Jeremy and Prestonwood Landscaping.

The next story is of a woman who was born to be a writer. From a young age, she wrote at every chance she got, finely crafting her skill into several published books as an adult. Nearly a decade ago, she built a business that would allow her to share her skills with other potential writers. One client led to another client, who referred a third, and soon, her schedule was packed as she tried to juggle the demands of helping so many authors craft their books. She's built a business from the ground up while working on her craft, taking care of her employees, and diligently maintaining a high-touch experience for her customers. Ten years is a lifetime in the entrepreneurial world, and she has shown the tenacity necessary to not just stay in business for that decade but to continually grow along the way.

But even with the success she's had, every new contract or promising idea is often met with skepticism in her mind. When I asked her about her hesitation, noting that her success was something she should be proud of, she spoke honestly about her experience. Having been raised in a fundamentalist religious culture with strict views on the role of women, she still felt the very distinct pressure "to find a good man, stay home, and have babies." Her willingness to be honest with herself and with me was admirable. Choosing to tell the truth was her first step to trading skepticism for optimism in her business and her mind. This is the story of my friend Allison Fallon, founder and creator of Find Your Voice.

The final story is about a friend who has found his purpose by helping others find theirs. He invites these seekers of truth to his office and diligently documents their life stories, uncovering clues that shed light on their core self. After several days together, he takes the raw material and helps create a road map for their life, giving them clarity and focus. But what truly sets him apart is the way he values honesty in the process—he refuses to let you stay where you are and gently pushes you toward your purpose.

He has been doing this work for years and has helped hundreds in their journeys. As demand has grown, he has grown a team of facilitators and developed a technology platform to document each process. There are hundreds of people in this world who have radically changed their lives because of this process and his willingness to *bear risk*. This is the story of Pete Richardson, the man who was instrumental in creating the Paterson Center and the LifePlan process.

I would argue that although Jeremy, Ally, and Pete may be lesser known than the Billy McFarlands, Elizabeth Holmeses, or Travis Kalanicks of the world, their contributions have made a more positive impact on the world. You may not find them on the cover of *Forbes* (yet!), but you will find them to be examples of leaders who chose a better way. A way that values the truth. A way that makes them Good Entrepreneurs.

END-OF-CHAPTER HOMEWORK
HOW DO YOU FIND TRUTH?

It is incredibly hard to tell the truth to someone else, and it is almost impossible to tell the truth to ourselves. For this reason, we need to ask for help from someone who knows us well. This person could be a spouse, partner, longtime friend, or sibling; choose someone who has witnessed your highest highs and lowest lows.

Once you have selected the person, ask them to reflect on the following questions regarding you. Ask them to take some time to really think about it, and tell them that you will be okay if they offend or shock you but that you need 100% honesty.

Then invite them to a coffee or drink in a private location, so that they can give you their answers. Your job is to act like a reporter by listening intently and asking clarifying questions. Don't be defensive; be *curious*.

Remember that this is only one person's opinion, and they may be projecting some of their own issues in their answers.

The questions are

- What is it like to be in a relationship with me?
- What is the best part of being in a relationship in with me?
- What is the worst part of being in a relationship with me?
- What is my superpower (the thing I do without even trying that is unique to me)?
- What is one thing I need to start doing?
- What is one thing that I need to stop doing?
- What do you want for my life?
- What question did I not ask that I should have?

While they reflect their answers back to you, make sure to write them down in your journal.

One final note, this is an incredibly hard exercise to complete, so if you are feeling scared or apprehensive, this is normal and a good sign to continue seeking truth in the midst of chaos.

PRINCIPLE FOUR

LEVERAGE DESPERATION TO FIND INSPIRATION

SOMEBODY'S LIFE IS ABOUT TO CHANGE

My daughter and I love watching love stories together. One of our all-time favorites is *Titanic*. Jane loves the movie because of the romance, but my favorite scene actually takes place at the opening of the movie.

The main character, Jack, is caught up in a card game, doubling down again and again until his friend, Fabrizio, leans over and warns him to not lose everything they have.

Jack's reply?

"When you got nothing, you got nothing to lose."[32]

The adversary across the table from Jack complains that his partner bet their tickets on the Titanic's maiden voyage.

Clearly, he has something to lose.

Clearly, somebody's life is about to change.

One by one, everyone begins to show their cards. Fabrizio and Olaf have no good cards. Sven has two pairs. All eyes move to Jack.

Jack looks at Fabrizio and apologizes.

Fabrizio quickly goes wild, exasperated about the money he thinks he just lost.

That is, until Jack cuts him off.

"I'm sorry you're not going to see your mom again for a long time. Because we're going to America!"[33]

DESPERATION AS A CATALYST

Over eighty percent of millionaires in America are first-generation millionaires.[34] Put another way, eight out of 10 millionaires did not start as millionaires, but they took risks and, in doing so, created additional wealth to join this elite club.

But although this statistic is impressive, you can't ignore the facts behind them.

The journey of entrepreneurship isn't easy. In fact, most of the time it will cause you to become desperate. And believe it or not, that's a good thing! Because it's in that moment of desperation that Good Entrepreneurs are born.

You've probably heard the phrase "necessity is the mother of invention." It's a proverb often attributed to Plato's *Republic*, where the B. Jowett translation states, "the true creator is necessity, who is the mother of our invention."[35]

In other words, out of our deep need can come our best creations. Our best inventions. Our best selves. When we find ourselves with nothing to lose, that's when we have everything to gain.

EMBRACE THE OBSTACLE

In Ryan Holiday's book *The Obstacle Is the Way*, he tells an old story about a king whose people had grown soft and entitled. In order to teach them a lesson, he placed a large boulder in the middle of the main road, blocking entry to the city.

The king hid and observed their reactions to this obstacle. Most of the subjects approached the rock and tried to move it but gave up after half-hearted attempts. Finally, a man approached the rock, and after not being able to move it, he refused to give up and found a large branch that he could use for leverage.

After using the branch to move the boulder, he found a stash of gold coins underneath and a note that said: "The obstacle in the path becomes the path. Never forget, within every obstacle is an opportunity to improve our condition."[36]

The wise king knew that the obstacle becomes the path. To try to get around it is to miss the journey entirely. Good Entrepreneurs know the same.

AN IDEA TO RISE

Every great business starts from one of the most precious resources in the world: an idea. You need lots of resources to make a business grow, but don't be confused—the idea is the most valuable of all because it provides the spark to begin the journey, and without it, you have nothing else. It starts with someone who wants to change something, or grow something, or become different. It starts with someone often who's frustrated with the status quo. It starts with someone who is desperate for difference. It's a life-changing process to be able to envision something that doesn't exist—to have an idea—and then see it through to fruition. This is the other side of desperation.

Before I ran my own business, I had the great fortune of being surrounded by many successful entrepreneurs. As a friend, an employee, and an investor, they allowed me to walk alongside them as they were growing their businesses. They shared what they'd learned and gained along the way, but most importantly, they opened up to me about their poor decisions and the consequences that followed.

While I was running RISE, I was surrounded by a team of people who were second to none. I always tried to hire people smarter than me and then get out of their way. I would tell my team, "Here is my bad idea; now make it better." And they would.

Good leaders don't operate on an island. They're surrounded by dozens of people who can help them execute their overall vision. They are supported by people who won't let their ideas die on the hill of desperation.

When I started RISE, I was desperate. At that point in my life, I had found some financial success but was exhausted from the lifestyle that came with it. At first, traveling for work was luxurious, but over time, I dreaded the trips. I had accumulated over two million miles on American Airlines in a decade, averaging over two hundred thousand miles a year. Most of those flights were domestic, which meant I was on the road almost every other week.

The travel experience was satisfactory about 50% of the time, bad about 40% of the time, and delightful just 10% of the time. Now, keep in mind, I was flying first-class almost all the time, and even up front, the experience was nothing to brag about. I know all the workers worked hard and wanted to give me a good experience, but the decks were stacked against them. Only internet service providers, subscription television companies, and health insurance companies score lower than airlines in customer satisfaction![37]

I remember being stuck in airports, delayed because of mechanical problems, and having to deal with frustrated flight attendants, and frustrated pilots, and frustrated front-desk staff, and frustrated security people, and frustrated passengers. Everybody I encountered during the process was frustrated.

And that doesn't even account for everything leading up to the flight! It was the parking in the overcrowded garage. It was standing in the line to get your ticket or check your bag. It was security—having to take off your shoes, take off your belt, and take off your jacket. It was making sure you didn't have any liquids over 3.4 ounces. It was getting to your gate and hopefully finding a decent cup of coffee and a bagel that was made sometime in the last three days. It was being herded like cattle to board the plane with the rest of the passengers.

It was such a difficult task to get from one city to another that the process left me desperate.

And when I finally had the opportunity to experience the difference of flying on a private plane, I had hope that I could continue to build businesses and be a good husband, father, and friend. I could have my cake and eat it too.

I found myself at this season of life with a beautiful wife and three beautiful children. They were growing up quickly, and I was missing soccer practice, rehearsals, school plays, opportunities to help out with homework. When I finally got home, I was so exhausted that I couldn't really engage. I knew that this was not the life that I wanted for myself or my family. It felt as if I was abandoning them. I had this massive hole in my heart from my dad being away in prison, and I was determined not to have my children feel the same way. I was desperate to give my family the life I wanted for us.

And so, I got an idea: I would buy a private plane.

Truth be told, the plane itself, although not inexpensive, wasn't the biggest obstacle. The management and flying of a private plane are often the more expensive and complicated pieces of the puzzle. That all added up to the realization that I shouldn't own a plane by myself. So, I wondered if I could get some friends to go in together. In my desperation to find a better way, I developed a bigger plan. What if I could share a private plane not just among my friends but with their friends, and their friends' friends?

I knew the market was large. I had inadvertently been doing market research for a decade, and I could see by looking at my fellow passengers on commercial flights that they were zombies. I could see it in their eyes. They hated it. They were pale. They were overweight. They didn't want to talk to anybody else. They were not excited to get on the plane. What started as an incredibly frustrating experience for me turned into an idea that birthed the dream that I could make a difference in that space.

Every product should be sold with one goal: to make the purchaser more successful than they were before they bought it. RISE was really started out of a desperate desire not to be away from my family as much as I had been. But if that could help other people too, why not take the risk? I was determined to find a way forward, and lucky for me, there were hundreds of thousands of other travelers who were desperate to find another way too.

When RISE launched, hardly a week went by when I wasn't getting a text, email, or voice mail from our members thanking us for the work we were doing. One customer sent me a picture of himself with his family at a restaurant with a text that said, "Because of RISE, I get to have dinner with my family tonight." That's when I knew we'd created something beautiful. From my desperation came something better, not just for me but for my friends, employees, and members.

That's what makes desperation so important for Good Entrepreneurs like you. Desperation is the father of creativity, and it's a key ingredient for your success as an entrepreneur. If you look at it this way, the dark moments and major obstacles will become one more step on the journey toward meaning and success. They can be the birthplace of some of your best ideas. But if you fail to see it as an opportunity, desperation will end your entrepreneurial journey before it even starts.

BORN FROM DESPERATION

So many of us take the wrong posture toward suffering. We try to avoid it, to ignore it, to get out of it at all costs. But when we do, we risk missing what can come from it. The attitude we take toward unavoidable suffering is one of the places we can find meaning in life. According to Victor Frankl in *Man's Search for Meaning*: "The meaning of life differs from man to man, from day to day and from hour to hour. What matters therefore is not the meaning of life in general, but rather the specific meaning of a person's life at a given moment."[38]

Struggles in life are not something to merely be *tolerated*; they can be great learning *opportunities*. Most people don't see it that way, and because of that, most people miss out on the great opportunity and education that desperate struggles can provide.

Think about this. What do all the following businesses have in common?

Fortune magazine
Federal Express

United Parcel Service
The Walt Disney Company
Hewlett-Packard Company
Charles Schwab Corporation
Standard Oil
Coors Brewing Corporation
Costco Wholesale Corporation
Revlon
General Motors Corporation
Procter & Gamble Company
United Airlines
Microsoft Corporation
LinkedIn

The answer? They followed the mantra of Rahm Emmanuel, Barack Obama's former chief of staff: "You never want a serious crisis to go to waste."[39]

All these businesses were started during an economic crisis or depression. They were born from a moment of desperation.

And the same can be true for you. Good Entrepreneurs let desperation be the push they need to take their next step. The job you hate? Let it motivate you to your next one. The tension you feel in your day-to-day frustrations? Let it be the reason you decide to come up with a solution. The desire you have to build a better community? Let it be the catalyst to your entrepreneurial journey, because Good Entrepreneurs aren't defeated by desperation.

A PUNCH IN THE MOUTH

In *The Hobbit* by J. R. R. Tolkien, the story invites the reader into the life of Bilbo Baggins, a reserved and home-loving hobbit who has a comfortable life. Everything is just the way he likes it, until a wizard named Gandalf tricks him into hosting a party for 13 dwarves who upend his home and, ultimately, his life. They convince him to go on a journey to defeat a dragon named Smaug. Along the way, the group encounters goblins and trolls.

They get separated from each other and find themselves in ever-more-desperate situations. This adventure allows the reader to follow the maturation of Bilbo Baggins, growing stronger with every encounter that challenges him. He's a stark contrast to the dwarves, who never seem to change from the beginning of the story till the end.[40]

I often think about Bilbo in the context of the entrepreneurial journey, realizing that the same themes apply to us as entrepreneurs. In the world of the entrepreneur, it's a little less fantastical, although it often doesn't feel any less daunting. In our journey, we must convince investors to back us, employees to quit their stable jobs to come work with us, and clients to give us their hard-earned money. We can hardly wait to get started, barely getting our foot out the door when something unexpected happens. Without seeing it coming, we run smack dab into trouble.

The German field marshal known as Moltke the Elder famously said, "No plan of operations extends with certainty beyond the first encounter with the enemy's main strength."[41]

Or, to make this even more simple, the philosopher Mike Tyson said, "Everyone has a plan until they get punched in the mouth."[42]

Everyone *thinks* they know what they're doing until they get started. Until they meet their first enemy and their first challenge. This is where the Good Entrepreneurs are separated from the posers.

This is where the real journey begins.

Andy Grove, the legendary management guru, said, "Bad companies are destroyed by crisis. Good companies survive them. Great companies are improved by them."[43] This was after his company took a 475-million-dollar charge against earnings for a recall of Intel processing chips. Talk about a punch in the mouth!

So, the question is when you get punched in the mouth, how will you react? One path leans into fear, frustration, anger, confusion, helplessness, or victimization. The other leans into desperation as the means for growth. One entrepreneur might stay down for the count. The Good Entrepreneur gets up and keeps swinging.

END-OF-CHAPTER HOMEWORK
HOW DO WE USE DESPERATION FOR GROWTH?

Take a minute and think about the last time you faced a challenge, either in your personal life or your professional life. A crisis. An obstacle in your path to getting something you wanted. What was your response? What did it bring up in you? How did it affect you? The way we respond tells us a lot about ourselves. Good Entrepreneurs see crisis as an opportunity for growth.

Growth is accelerated when you are clear and focused. Recreate the following table in your journal and then follow the instructions below to create a simple way to target what you want to address and move ahead on.

Growth Areas Table

Category	Broken to Good	Good to Great	Great to Optimized
Personal			
Professional			

The rows represent the two primary areas of life: personal (relationship, behavioral, and emotional challenges) and professional (career, job, and work challenges). The three columns represent the possible levels to grow in:

- ☛ Broken to good: There is a struggle in the area that you would like to resolve.

- Examples of personal: a marriage issue; a parenting problem; a troublesome bad habit that is not going away; disruptive emotions that get in your way

- Examples of professional: a leadership problem; strategic concerns; systems or financial issues; inability to find your niche

☞ Good to great: Things are going well, but you could use improvement.

- Examples of personal: a lack of passion for what you are doing; a feeling of stagnation in your marriage; unexciting dating life; a lack of fulfillment in what you are engaged in

- Examples of professional: slow growth in the organization; few opportunities to excel

☞ Great to optimized: Things are going very well, but you want to be optimizing matters toward your true potential.

- Examples of personal: kids need to be more focused on their potential; you're in good physical condition, but you want to optimize it; you are happy but want more joy.

- Examples of professional: you want to be at the peak of your skills and passions; you want to the be the best leader possible.

Unless you do not want to have goals, it's simply impossible to not have anything in these cells that matters to you. Identify what the challenge is that you want to work on.

PRINCIPLE FIVE

MAKE INTENTIONAL DECISIONS

THE DECISIONS THAT WILL CHANGE YOUR LIFE

What if I told you that the difference between the successful life you dream of and one of the most devastating lives you could possibly imagine was shaped from only a handful of decisions? *I believe it's between five and 10 key decisions that determine your legacy.* That might sound inspiring to you, or it might sound terrifying, but the purpose we're craving in our personal lives and in our work can be shaped and marked by just a few key decisions.

Think about it:

- Who you choose to partner with or marry
- The choice to take the easy route or the path of integrity
- The quick fix or the long haul
- Speaking your truth or holding your breath

- Asking for what you need or pretending to be fine
- Living in community and choosing to being seen
- To take a risk or stay the same.

This might seem shocking to you or even unbelievable, but I promise it's true. And it's why intentional decision-making is key for Good Entrepreneurs. Let's take a look at a couple of key decisions that determined the legacy of three individuals.

Sometimes the outcomes of these decisions take decades to manifest themselves, and my friend Patrick Soon-Shiong is the perfect example of this. He owns the *Los Angeles Times*, is part owner of the LA Lakers and has a portfolio of incredible companies. Although he enjoys the finer things in life now, his start in life was very different. He grew up in South Africa under apartheid and had to fight to be the first non-White doctor admitted to a "Whites-only" medical school. He and his wife emigrated to North America with only a few thousand dollars and followed his passion of medical research.

In 1985, Soon-Shiong was trying to pioneer transplanting cells from pigs to humans when he discovered a virus in the pigs that could harm the patients.[44] He refused to proceed and was sued by his investors but later won in arbitration.

Fast-forward to 2008, and the U.S. supply of the blood thinner heparin became tainted, and over 55 people died from these issues. Among other uses, heparin is used during dialysis treatment to prevent the blood from clotting in systems while it is being treated outside the body. Without access to it, most dialysis patients would suffer.

During this crisis, Patrick owned APP Pharmaceuticals, one of several suppliers of heparin approved by the Food & Drug Administration (FDA). But more importantly, it was the only supplier that could prove their heparin was not tainted. How? Because the raw material for heparin comes from pigs. Patrick's experience with pigs two decades prior allowed him to make the intentional decision of owning the entire supply chain, starting with the live pigs to ensure they were virus-free.

Despite protest from investors and experts in the industry, he held fast, and his intentional decision was rewarded when he sold APP Pharmaceuticals in July of 2008 to Fresenius SE for $4.6 billion.[45] Since Fresenius was one of the largest dialysis providers in the U.S., they needed to ensure they had access to heparin to continue their work. Patrick provided the answer to their need. And even though he had to wait decades to reap the benefits of his intentional decision, when he finally did, it made him a billionaire, and more importantly, it saved the lives of countless people.

Most of us know that Amelia Earhart was the first woman to make a transatlantic flight.[46] But because she was female, she was initially thought to be too frail to be a pilot, so she took a job as a social worker instead. But she made the key decision to keep looking for an opportunity to fly. After numerous attempts, she was finally offered the funding for the flight, but there was a catch. She wouldn't fly by herself. Instead, she would go with two men as chaperones. Not only that, but the men would also be paid while she would fly without pay.

She could've declined the offer that was well below her ideal, but she made the decision to do what was necessary to keep going. She took the first step, and she didn't wait for the opportunity to be perfect. A few years later, she became the first woman to fly solo nonstop across the Atlantic, and because of that, we still talk about her today. The day she made the decision to say yes changed the course of history and removed a block from the wall of patriarchy.

For Phil Knight, the founder of Nike, the first several years of his business were a roller coaster. He knew his idea of building the best running shoes in the world could be great, but first he had to get through a few days that could've sunk him completely. He writes in his book *Shoe Dog* about one day when several creditors showed up at Nike headquarters looking for answers.

"Folks—we're going to Code Red. This building, this 4,500-square-foot building, is about to be swarming with people to whom we owe money. Whatever else we do today, we cannot let any of them bump into each other." Every entrepreneur I know has been in a similar position at some point.

Knight continued, "If they cross paths in the hall, if one unhappy creditor meets another unhappy creditor, and if they should have a chance to compare notes, they will freak out. They could team up and decide on some sort of collaborative payment schedule! Which would be Armageddon."[47]

They created a plan assigning a Nike employee to each creditor to keep an eye on them and to escort them through the building. Phil had to scurry between creditors trying to find a way to survive another day. In the end, the plan worked, each creditor walked away committed to keep going, and most importantly, none of them met each other!

If those creditors, who were literally feet away from each other, had run into each other on that fateful day, we wouldn't know the name Nike.

These decisions determined everything for Patrick, Amelia, and Phil.

And they can for you too. Good Entrepreneurs have to be aware of the decisions they make. They have to make decisions with purpose and intention. Because I'm here to tell you from personal experience that just a few decisions can determine if you end up in the private plane or the prison cell.

What if you knew that you were just a few key decisions away from the life you've most dreamed of? Or the one you most fear? Wouldn't you take your choices more seriously? Wouldn't you want to have a system for making even the small decisions in your life more intentionally? Wouldn't it give you a little more courage to make the decision you knew was right, even if others disagreed with you?

Most of us don't think of our daily decisions this way. Maybe we should.

AN OBITUARY

Oddly enough, the time most of us spend reflecting on our decisions isn't when we're in the midst of making them. It's when it's all said and done—when we're at the end of the road—that we look back at the choices that have led us to where we've ended up. The average human will live to the age of 73.[48] That means that we have over 26,000 days to make decisions that will help us craft a life of meaning.

The reason I had you begin to write your obituary in chapter two is because an obituary has a way of removing all the static that lives in our head. In the same way that Samuel Johnson said, "Depend upon it, sir, when a man knows he is to be hanged in a fortnight, it concentrates his mind wonderfully,"[49] my friend Don Miller turned me on to reviewing my obituary, and I can attest it does have a wonderful effect on focusing my head for the day ahead. In fact, read any obituary. Although the people who are written about there had thousands of opportunities to make meaningful lives, what's remembered in the end is usually no more than a handful of days.

The reality is that most of life is lived in the shadows. People go through the motions of their lives, doing things that will never be seen, much less remembered, by anyone else. But your big decisions—as invisible as they are—can and do lead to big moments that everyone remembers in the end. Take for example the 11th chapter from the book of Hebrews in the Bible. In it, we find a list of leaders like Abel, Noah, Abraham, Isaac, Jacob, Joseph, Moses, and Rahab, "the Jericho harlot" (yep, there is a sex worker in there). By each of their names, the author lists one thing that person did that defined their lives (Hebrews 11, MSG). One choice they made that changed everything. Decisions we still talk about today.

Pretty cool, right?

What choices are going to define you in the end?

One day, I sat down, opened the paper, and came across *The New York Times* obituary of William Sokolin. The title almost caused me to drop my coffee.

"William Sokolin, Wine Seller Who Broke Famed Bottle, Dies at 85."[50] Of course, I continued reading.

"The slightest mishap can cause someone to cry over their beer or shed tears over spilled milk, but on April 23, 1989, at the Four Seasons restaurant in Manhattan, nobody could have blamed William Sokolin if he had sobbed over a broken bottle of wine."[51]

On that fateful night, Mr. Sokolin accidentally bumped into a metal-topped tray table and knocked two holes into his historic smoky-green bottle. The bottle Mr. Sokolin famously broke that night was a Château

Margaux that was rumored to have belonged to Thomas Jefferson, and Mr. Sokolin had been hoping to sell it for $519,750.

The obituary continued to give additional details of his life, but it also dove into more details of his infamous wine mishap. Mr. Sokolin beat the average human being by living 31,000 days, and the summation of those days was a headline about the day he had one mishap.

I'm not saying this to make you feel depressed. But I *am* wanting you to think about how important your choices are. *There are no mistakes in life, there are only decisions and the consequences that stem from them.*

How many of us can relate to the feeling that one decision might define us forever? The reality is it could happen to any of us. But the way to avoid this is to become intentional about our decisions—to get crystal clear about what our purpose is so that we don't miss a single opportunity to live it out. Sure, we might still make a decision that we have a hard time living down. But when we're clear about our purpose, even our consequences can be used to fulfill it.

The truth is we're all one defining decision away from being remembered as the person who sold the bottle of wine for hundreds of thousands of dollars or the person who broke it on the floor of a hotel. I don't know about you, but I want to do everything in my power to make sure I'm the former.

When I was in college, I saw a headline in the local paper that read "3 Who Stole Traffic Signs Sentenced to 15 Years."[52] These three friends stole a stop sign and were convicted of manslaughter after a Mack truck smashed into a car and killed three teenagers at the spot where the sign should have been. My heart sank when I read the article. I thought to myself, *How many nights did I spend as a teenager stealing street signs with my friends?* Snagging a stop sign gave you top marks in our game. And how easily could those decisions have sent me to the place I was trying to avoid the most: prison?

"I don't believe for one minute that you or the other two defendants pulled these signs up with the intent of causing the death of anyone," Judge Joe Anderson Mitcham told the defendants. "But pulling up the signs has caused ramifications that none of you may have ever expected."[53]

Our decisions, big and small, are the difference makers. They have ramifications, for better or for worse, that we may never expect. And because of that, if we want to be Good Entrepreneurs, we must make decisions with intention.

MAKING THE MOST OF BAD DECISIONS

One of the best questions you can ask yourself is this:

What do I want to be known for?

Your answer to that will help you determine the direction you want to take. It will help you define the decisions you need to make to get there.

My friend Mike is full of kindness and generosity and would literally give a stranger the shirt off his back. But he became known to the public for just two days in his life.

First, he is famous for being the pitcher that gave up a record-breaking home run (#756) to Barry Bonds in 2007.[54]

Mike is one of the most competitive people I know. Even when we go on vacation together, he is in a rush to be the first to the top of the mountain on a hike. So, I know that when he gave up that home run, he was crushed to have had his name sealed in history as the person who lost that battle with Barry Bonds. But if you go back and look at the interviews he gave that night and even over the next several days, Mike was gracious, level headed, and represented the real man I know and love. The decision to be a good sportsman in the moment caused Mike to be known as a gracious competitor.

Even when he lost!

But the second thing Mike is known for is a slipup on social media. In the heat of the battle with the San Antonio Spurs, Mike's beloved Dallas Mavericks were getting beaten in the playoffs. At a bar with a few friends and after maybe too much beer, he tweeted out a phrase that was derogatory and despicable.[55] The fact that it was used regularly as an audio drop on the radio station he worked at then provided no excuse in the moment. Before public record existed online, it would've been said into the ether and gone away in a moment. But now, with thousands of followers to see it, Mike was responsible for the words in a new way. He was fired from his job and found himself a man without an island. Then, he became known as someone else completely.

One man. Two choices. Both with the potential to affect his life. One was made with intention, one a fleeting impulse.

And still, both are the kind that can mark a legacy.

Thankfully, Mike knows how much decisions matter, so he decided not to let that one remark ruin him. Since then, he's made a public apology to those he hurt. He takes his role as a leader more seriously now and is much more likely to speak up when someone else is saying something unkind than he was before all this. Not a day passes that Mike doesn't think about the importance of his words, especially the words he puts online.

See, even when we choose the wrong decisions, they don't have to be wasted.

TRUST THE PROCESS

So how do we prepare for these potentially momentous days if we don't even know when they are coming? How do we prepare for the decisions that will make or break us if we don't even know how to recognize them when they're happening?

The answer isn't easy, but it is simple. You make an intentional decision to trust the process. Start there. Lean into the process that will help you become the Good Entrepreneur you want to be. Decide to trust that each step will help you get to where you want to go. And then do it.

What exactly is that process? Well, I think it's defined in five steps.

1. Win the morning.

    The time between when the sun comes up and when you first interact with technology is precious time. When we sleep, we enter a dream world full of possibilities. The moment we look at our calendar, social media, or email, we switch over to the pragmatic side of our brains and most likely lose our creative potential until the next day. That's why Good Entrepreneurs must decide to *win the morning*. When I wake up, I spend time meditating. I focus on what's happening in my mind. Once I have spent time reflecting on my thoughts, I open my journal (always Moleskine), review my obituary, write down my daily mantra, and spend about 15 minutes writing, free of any other thoughts. This process, which takes about 30 minutes, is my rudder for the day. It sets me up to be as prepared as possible for the tasks at hand. Of course, to win the morning, you must decide to do so not just when you wake up but when you go to sleep the night before. I try to get to bed at a sensible time and like to sleep with my blinds open so that I can rise with the sun. Think about what a win in the morning would look like for you. Then, make the decision to do it!

2. Think about the task at hand.

   Nick Saban, the head coach of the University of Alabama football team, is known for marching to the beat of his own drum. He doesn't worry about what other coaches are focused on. He just worries about the task at hand. He famously says to his team: "Don't think about winning the SEC Championship. Don't think about the National Championship. Think about what you need to do in this drill, in this play, in this moment. That's the process. Let's think about what we can do today, the task at hand."[56] The decision to focus on the task at hand has taken his teams to six national championships. And those wins started with one decision. So how can you shift your thinking to do the same, focusing on the task at hand, one choice at a time?

3. Establish boundaries.

   Having good boundaries is the key to healthy relationships. But the tricky thing about boundaries is that you cannot force others to establish them. You can only establish them yourself. You must decide to be the one who sets boundaries that work for you. *Bound-*

aries, by Henry Cloud and John Townsend, has sold two million copies and continues to be a bestseller, despite being released 30 years ago.[57] That's because these guys hit a nerve. They tapped into the importance of boundaries. They share what it means for you to stand up and claim your own agency regardless of the request from the other person. When you have good boundaries, you put yourself in a better position to make each day successful. Making the decision to establish solid boundaries with the people in your life will help you protect your time, energy, and resources. It will help you stay the course of the Good Entrepreneur.

4. Prepare, don't hustle.

There is a saying in the startup world that goes "The dream is free. The hustle is sold separately." I have seen this sign hung up in many offices I've visited with friends and clients. I understand the sentiment of the phrase, but if I'm honest, I absolutely hate it. Because if you're making decisions that will help you get where you want to go, then you don't need to hustle nearly as much as you think you do. It's just like how in the corporate world, there is an inverse relationship between how hard you work and how much you get paid. The first-year associate at a consulting firm works much harder than the partner but gets paid far less. Why is that? Because the experience of the partner makes them more efficient and valuable (or at least it should!). The more intentional you are in your decision-making, the more efficient you'll be in your work. And the more efficient you are in your work, the less hustle your work will require. So, prepare yourself now by looking at where you've come from in your journey, where you are now, and where you want to be. Remove the need for hustle so that you can strategically make decisions to affect your long-term goals. Work smarter, not harder.

5. Do your job.

I remember a phone call I had with my dad when I was in college. I wanted to drop a class that I wasn't doing well in because I was lazy, and he gave me a talking to from prison that I will never forget.

"Nick, you have a job to do, and that job is to do your best in school. I don't care what grade you get if you do your best. My job in here is to clean up the dumpster area behind the kitchen. You've never seen such a disgusting place in your life! But I made up my mind that if that was my job, I was going to make it the best. It would be the cleanest I could possibly make it. And it's so clean now that the other guys in the unit come outside just to gawk at it."

It doesn't matter what your job is. If it's to make lunches in the morning for your kids, or file paperwork at the office, or lead a team of people, or clean the dumpster area in a prison, Good Entrepreneurs make the decision to do their jobs well. They do it to the best of their ability. Because they know that how they do the littlest job is how they're going to do the largest job. No matter what the task is, deciding to do it well is a key intentional decision for any Good Entrepreneur.

THE CONSEQUENCES YOU CREATE

It's important to note here that although making intentional decisions is a huge piece of the puzzle of success, it's not a guarantee. In fact, as an entrepreneur facing new situations every day, the only guarantee is that you will have to manage consequences along the way. And honestly, some of them will be big ones.

In my own life, I have made so many poor decisions that have led to negative consequences that it's hard to choose which one to share. The most recent bad decision came in the form of a Porsche 911 Turbo. I purchased the car, and I made the most out of the genius of the German engineers. Like a moron, I did it on a public road and was swiftly pulled over by a Texas state trooper. When I came to a stop, I rolled down my window to receive a healthy dose of reality.

"If it wasn't for COVID and me wanting to protect my family, I would haul you into jail," the officer said.

My speeding had no excuse. Racing (and beating) an Audi R8 was dumb and immature and had put my life and that of others in jeopardy. After seeking and receiving counsel from my friends Scott and David, I returned home that night, thankful to have avoided a tragedy. I told Angela that I was selling the car, realizing I didn't need access to a car that fast. This day could have been one to determine my life trajectory, but friends' counsel provided a safe landing. They helped me turn a bad decision into a better outcome.

Good Entrepreneurs know that just as quickly as one decision can break you, the next decision after that can repair you.

REDEMPTION

The day after my friend Mike sent his infamous tweet, I was boarding a ferry in Washington when I called him to check in. He was being disciplined by the radio station and was heartbroken to have made such a bad decision. He recognized his error and vowed to never do it again. Through tears, he confessed his frustration, not because of the discipline from his employer but rather because of the embarrassment and pain he had brought on his wife, children, parents, coworkers, and even those he didn't know who were hurt by his tweet. The Mike I knew was doing exactly what I have known him to do for the better part of two decades: taking care of those he loved.

While I sat on the ferry passing by Bainbridge Island, Mike and I talked about how our worst decisions do not define us. They may be all that most people who do not love us will remember about us, but those who don't love us don't get to define us. We have to decide to lean into those who *do* love us because they're the ones who will hold us up. They're the ones who will point us toward redemption.

Mike did exactly that. He found redemption in his story, and he has refused to let those days define him since. Those of us who love him hardly remember that day.

For me, the most significant days of my life can be counted on two hands.

- The day I found out my father was arrested.
- The day nobody died after I stole a stop sign in high school.
- The day I almost died on I-70 in the Rocky Mountains.
- The day that I got a call from a baseball coach in Arkansas offering me a scholarship.
- The day that I met Calvin Howe (chapter six), my surrogate father.
- The day I gathered the courage to ask Angela out on a first date.
- The days my children were born.
- The day I met a billionaire, who took me under his wing and mentored me.
- The day I got so frustrated with American Airlines that I decided to go for broke and create something better.
- The day my other surrogate father, Richard Hoffman (chapter 12), allowed me to see the truth about myself and let me knock myself down after "I had set myself up."

I can say, without a doubt, these moments changed the trajectory of my life. The decisions I made before and after each moment have helped take my life from the prison waiting room to a life of meaning.

What would your most significant days be?

Take some time to list them.

The mark of the Good Entrepreneur is to live a life of meaning. To do that, we must make intentional decisions that get us there. We have to hold both the negative and positive consequences of our life together, so we can learn, trust the process, and intentionally decide to keep going.

END-OF-CHAPTER HOMEWORK
THE DAYS THAT DEFINE US

Take out your journal, review the obituary that you wrote, and answer these questions:

- What are the days you mentioned in your obituary?
- What days that define you were left out of your obituary?
- What days that haven't happened yet will define your life?
- What would you change as you edit your obituary?

Don't rush this process—take some time to reflect on your life and the lives of the people whom you respect. Then go back to the obituary and update it with your new thoughts from this chapter.

PRINCIPLE SIX

ASK FOR HELP

IT'S LONELY AT THE TOP

As people who strive to become better and do better, it's tempting to believe the lie that you have to do it all on your own—that you have to beat out the competition, outperform your peers, make a name for yourself, and stake your claim at the top.

As I've walked the path of the entrepreneur, I've felt this way and ended up isolated and paranoid. But you know what I've realized? It doesn't have to be lonely at the top.

Good Entrepreneurs know they don't have to do it on their own. And in fact, they know they can't!

NO LONE WOLVES

Human beings are designed to need help.

For years, I thought this was one of our weaknesses. That's because I wanted to be the lone wolf. I would proudly tell others that I had pulled myself up by my own bootstraps. I did it all on my own, and to me, those were bragging rights. But now I see how truly naive that mindset really was because, from the beginning of time, human beings were made for community. It's part of the rhythm of our world, and it's a big part of my story.

It starts at birth. Humans are born before they can fend for themselves. A cow can trot shortly after birth, a bird can fly within a few weeks of hatching, and a puppy leaves its mother to explore a mere month after birth. But human babies are essentially helpless, dependent for many years on others for food, shelter, protection, and education.

When I'm sick, I go to a doctor because I need help beyond my own knowledge. The doctor, in turn, uses their training and years of cumulative knowledge to diagnose and treat me. If I tried to be the lone wolf in my medical care, I might be dead.

A governing board is set up in an organization for the same reason. It is designed to be an objective body that can see the blind spots of a company and its executives in order to help guide them. It doesn't run the company daily. Instead, the board meets together every few months to review progress and provide guidance. Its job is to save the company from disaster and help it thrive. If companies tried to operate as lone wolves without entities like governing boards, they'd be left without support, accountability, or a team to have their back. (Look at what happened at Theranos when its board didn't provide oversight for its executives.)

Before a plane takes off, there is a team of maintenance workers who ensure the plane is flightworthy. They follow the FAA-approved manufacturer guidelines to inspect the plane. These guidelines lay out very specific rules based on the number of hours flown, the number of landings made, and many more flight-based metrics. When the maintenance is performed, it is logged in a book that is assigned to that specific plane. It provides a record of all the work done to show the plane is maintained appropriately and safe to fly. Rarely do passengers meet these mechanics, and often the pilots don't either. But without them, the plane wouldn't be airworthy. They work quietly behind the scenes to make sure that air travel isn't a lone (and therefore dangerous!) experience.

The list could go on and on. Yet many entrepreneurs I know have no formal team in place to support and enable their superpowers. Worse yet, this lone-wolf attitude is reinforced in the glowing stories we tell about entrepreneurs, lifting them up as if they did everything all by themselves.

Good Entrepreneurs know better. They know there is no such thing as a lone wolf in this world. And because of that, they value surrounding themselves with the right people. They hire others who are better than themselves. They build teams who can support their visions and make them reality. They aren't intimidated or threatened by others; instead, they're empowered by them.

This is the paradox of being an entrepreneur. On the one hand, you need to march to the beat of your own drum. On the other, you're dead in the water if you try to go alone.

As Steve Jobs famously said in his 2005 Stanford commencement address, "Your time is limited, so don't waste it living someone else's life. Don't be trapped by dogma—which is living with the results of other people's thinking. Don't let the noise of others' opinions drown out your own inner voice. And most important, have the courage to follow your heart and intuition."[58]

This man put a dent in the universe. He's often held up as an überentrepreneur.

But the reality is that Steve Jobs wasn't a lone wolf. He had an army of 20,000 people behind him. There were teams upon teams that helped him with every aspect of his company. They vetted his intuition, made models to determine viability, and provided pushback when necessary. In the world of any successful entrepreneur, even the loneliest lone wolf is more of a myth than reality.

WARNING LIGHTS

When we deny the reality that we need people—both in business and in life—we move faster and faster toward a crash. If we pay attention, there are always warning lights, telling us we're in danger along the way: warnings about burnout, warnings about questionable decisions, and warnings about our ego getting in the way. Those warnings are a gift that too often go unopened.

About three months into flying scheduled services with RISE, I was finally starting to let other people in the company worry about the minute details of the schedule. One Thursday, I arrived home exhausted and made myself a rye Manhattan, my favorite medication to numb the ails of the day. I was a few sips into my drink when my chief operating officer called. I let it go to voice mail. Whatever it was, it could wait till tomorrow. But when he quickly called a second time, I saw the warning lights. I took the call.

"Nick, we've had an aborted takeoff in Austin. Everyone is safe, but we are gathering the details right now. Please call into the emergency conference number so that we can discuss the appropriate response."

I quickly sobered up and dialed in. Our last flight of the day had taken off from Austin and was en route to Dallas when an engine light indicating oil pressure loss had flashed on. The pilots, following procedure, shut down the engine to try to prevent any additional issues.

Most people think that flying on a plane with two engines is safer than one. That thought process makes sense. If you have one engine and it breaks, then you have no engines. But if you have two engines and you lose one, you can still fly on the remaining engine. However, if you ask any professional pilot, they will tell you that if an untrained pilot loses one engine, the plane will flip over, and the remaining engine will get you to the crash site faster.

Luckily, in this situation, our professionally trained pilots knew what to do. They made a loop back to Bergstrom airport with one engine and were greeted by the emergency crew as they approached the runway. The plane was towed back to the hangar, and the passengers and pilots got off the plane and safely into the terminal. Crisis averted.

When the investigation was complete on the plane, it turned out that the engine was fine. It wasn't a mechanical failure in the plane; it was an error with the warning light. There was no reason to shut down the engine, but the pilots didn't know that at the time. They followed the warning signs because that's what they're trained to do.

Shortly after this episode, I was in Hollywood driving my friend's Volkswagen Karmann Ghia late at night up Benedict Canyon. We took it out for a quick run just to see how it would feel since it had been 20 years since I had driven one (my first car). On the way down the canyon, everything was working fine. But on the way back up, we started to smell the scent of burning oil. Liam brought it to my attention, but I assured him it was only the smell of a 40-year-old VW powering up the hill. It was a smell I knew well, and because of that, I ignored the "warning lights" from the car. But as I pulled into his driveway, the entire back of the car exploded in flames. We were safe, but the car would not live to see another day.

I think about this incident frequently. So often in my life, I've ignored warning lights, refusing to shut down the engine and return to the airport and instead powering on, believing that one engine was enough to get me to my destination. In fact, often when I knew I was in danger, I would ignore or even remove the warning lights completely. I'd isolate myself from the people who I knew would question my decisions and my motives—friends and family members who knew my tendencies and could sit me down to have hard conversations. People who would flash warning lights in my life. That's because those warning lights were too inconvenient. They would slow me down. They'd keep me from getting to my desired destination on my time frame.

But let me ask you this: Can you make it to your desired destination if your vehicle explodes while you're on your way? There's a *reason* we have warning lights and a reason that protocol insists we listen to them, no matter why we believe they're going off. The reason is clear: they may save us from destruction.

The moral of the story is this: be like the pilots, not like me.

It doesn't matter what you *feel* about a situation. It matters what the warning lights are saying.

The lauded psychiatrist Elvin Semrad taught us this: "The greatest sources of our suffering are the lies we tell ourselves."[59] I know from personal experience that this is true. You probably do too. And one of the biggest lies I've believed is that warning lights would hold me back. Because the reality is those warning lights in our lives flash for a reason—a good reason. We just can't always see that reason on our own.

The people in your life whom you love, who are of sound mind, who care about you, and who have your back—your spouse, your children, your mentors, your peer leaders—they are your warning lights. When they're all "flashing," telling you the same thing at once, my admonition to you is listen to them.

Or you might just end up calling 911.

911

Ron is one of my clients who lives in another state. (I've changed his name for anonymity reasons, but his story is true.) We meet in person several times a year, and in between, we have video calls. There are several long-term goals that he is working on in both his career and his personal life that I'm helping him with as we go.

On one call with Ron, I could tell something was wrong. His face was pale, and his eyes were bloodshot. He had postponed several of our calls already, which is what usually happens when someone needs to discuss something uncomfortable. One look at him on that video screen confirmed what I suspected. Something was up with Ron.

I start all my calls with my clients by asking the same question: do you have any 911s?

This is intended to move the big item that is derailing everything else to the front of the call. It's designed to help them bring it right up and deal with it. Ripping the Band-Aid™ off isn't always the right move, but often, it's necessary to snap us to attention appropriately.

With Ron, I barely got the 911 question out of my mouth before he responded.

"Nick, I am in a bit of crisis, and I don't know what to do. My wife took the kids to visit her family. She was supposed to be gone for two weeks, and that was three months ago. We've been in a rough patch for most of our fifteen years of marriage, but this is the worst it has ever been."

This happened in the middle of the COVID-19 crisis. He and his wife reasoned that a rural location was better for their kids during that time than the populated city they lived in. However, now Ron wanted to see his kids. He wanted his family back at home and he wanted his marriage together.

I responded carefully. "Wow, that is a lot to handle, Ron. I'm sorry to hear the stress that you are dealing with, and I am thankful that you have chosen to tell me the truth of the situation."

"You haven't heard the worst part," he continued. "Our oldest daughter is not my child, and she doesn't know it. My wife was unfaithful in our first year of marriage, and she got pregnant."

Do you want to know what's amazing about the human brain? It is never at rest. We are always sensing, imaging, dreaming, fretting, or acting out possible scenarios in our lives. A neuron by itself can't do much, but when 86 billion of them work in concert, we can produce greatness, like John Coltrane's *A Love Supreme*, Elon Musk's SpaceX, or the mapping of the human genome. Or we can produce our own personal hell. For a decade, Ron's brain had been doing mostly the former—helping him climb the corporate ladder and achieve incredible success. Now it had turned on him, doing the latter.

Unchecked, our brains can torment our lives.

Through sobs, Ron continued. "Every time I want a change in our marriage that my wife doesn't want, she threatens to tell my kids. My kids are my life. If they knew I wasn't there biological father, it would ruin them."

"Ron, you have two options, and neither of them is pain-free," I told him. "The first is to stop the lying and begin to tell the truth. This will bring on a rush of acute pain that will seem to be too much, but I can promise you, you'll make it through, given enough time. The second option is to do nothing. If you choose this route, tomorrow you will wake up, and your pain will be ever so slightly worse. And the day after that, it will be slightly worse. You will try to numb it with accolades, or alcohol, or any number of other things, but it will be there. It will stay below the surface ready to explode at the most inopportune time."

I paused to give him time to consider before continuing. "Here's the deal. Your kids are going to find out that you aren't perfect, and the longer it takes for them to come to that truth, the worse it will be when they do. The ball is in your court to make a decision."

He responded. "The current situation is no longer tenable. I need to make a change. What do I do?"

"Tell the truth," I responded.

LIVING IN COMMUNITY

Good Entrepreneurs surround themselves with the right influence. They choose to invite people who make things better all-around into their lives and their work.

So, if you want to be a Good Entrepreneur (And I think you do! I mean, you've made it this far in the book.), you must look honestly at the people you've invited to participate in your life. Ask yourself:

- Are they making me better?
- Are they stretching me to push forward even when it's uncomfortable?
- Are they holding me accountable to the standards I espouse?
- Are they safe to hold my deepest, darkest secrets confidentially?
- Are they building me up or dragging me down?

This is so important because who you spend your time with has an influence on who you will become. Don't be ashamed to need help. You have a journey to accomplish, and you will need help from many along the way. So be intentional about finding the kind of people who will help you and who will spur you on toward becoming the kind of entrepreneur—the kind of person—you want to be.

THE TRIANGLE OF LIFE

How do you do that exactly? Well, I think every Good Entrepreneur needs to have three types of people in their lives—a mentor, a mentee, and a mensch—to create what I call the triangle of life.

Mentor. Mentee. Mensch.

Each role has a specific purpose and associated tasks. Whereas my mensches walk through life beside me, my mentors are people who have already walked the path where I am headed. They prepare me for what's ahead while I, in turn, help my mentees, the third point of the triangle, by guiding them on their own journeys.

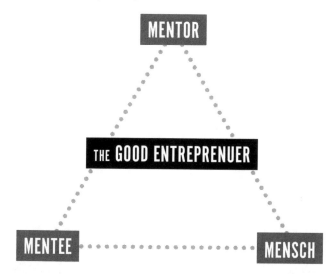

Good Entrepreneurs operate in this triangle. You may be impressive as a lone wolf, but can you build and grow your business on your own? It's possible. But you will only be more successful if you bring people around you.

HOW TO BE A MENTOR

On a cool fall morning of my freshman year of college, Jim Carr, the Executive Vice President (EVP) of Harding University, walked by. I waved to him, and he waved back before abruptly stopping and motioning for his walking companion to follow him. They were headed in my direction.

"Good morning, Nick. I'd like to invite you to meet someone very important to me. This is Calvin Howe."

To meet Calvin was to love Calvin. He was short, impeccably dressed, and when he smiled, his eyes seemed to disappear almost as if his cheeks swallowed them whole. He had very little hair on his head, and he was almost always smiling. It was like looking into the face of an emoji. You couldn't help but smile back at this wonderful man who was small in stature but giant in character.

"Calvin, this is Nick Kennedy. He's the student I was telling you about."

Wait, why was Jim Carr telling this man something about me? And what could he possibly be telling him?

"Oh, I see," Calvin replied. "Tell me a little about yourself, Nick."

In that moment, Calvin was thoughtful, kind, and present, almost as if he had been on the way to meet me specifically. I remember feeling comfortable in his presence. So, when he extended an invitation to lunch with him, I accepted right away.

Through Jim, Calvin had heard about my dad and wanted to know how he could help. He was always asking how he could help.

After those initial meetings, Calvin became a surrogate father to me. Anything he had, he offered to me. He invited me to his lake house and gave me free rein when I was there, including the use of his boat and jet skis. I would show up, often with a friend in tow, and Lois, Calvin's kind and gracious wife, would immediately start to feed us and give us iced tea or lemonade. I could talk to Calvin about anything. He always felt present and never rushed, always ready to listen and share his time and resources generously with me.

He counseled me on what jobs to take and what investments to make and impressed on me the importance of time. Calvin stood in the gap for me and helped me navigate some of life's toughest decisions.

He never told me outright what to do, but instead, he spoke in parables—parables that I still play through my head today.

One of the best life lessons he taught me had to do with knowing when to say *enough* by creating "your number"—that is, what is the amount of wealth you would like to have in your wildest dreams. Calvin and Lois decided early on in their marriage what amount of wealth they wanted to have and committed to give away everything after they reached that point. They had plenty of money, multiple homes, and successful businesses, but they also had a map of the United States that contained dozens of colored dots, representing the organizations that they helped through donations and other resources. They wanted for nothing, and their generosity was life changing to thousands of people.

Cultivate a superpower of knowing when to say enough. Just because you can doesn't mean you should.

Every Good Entrepreneur needs a Calvin. And every Good Entrepreneur needs to find a way to be a Calvin to someone else.

A good mentor will have the ability to:

1. **Listen.** People are constantly communicating—sometimes they even use words!
2. **Strip away everything that doesn't matter.** Focus is necessary to allocate our limited resources wisely.
3. **Be a professional question asker.** In order to get the right answers, you have to ask the right questions.
4. **Provide perspective.** Give perspective to your mentee based on the path you have previously walked.
5. **Tell stories.** We don't remember presentations; we remember stories.

HOW TO BE A MENTEE

While Calvin was investing in me, he asked me to invest as well. But since I didn't know what I didn't know, he simply asked me to be intentional in our relationship, reminding me that he would do whatever he could to help but that I needed to ask for the help.

He forced me to be a critical thinker, stripping away all that didn't matter and getting to the core issues. He did this by constantly asking me why. As in "Calvin, I am thinking about taking this job with a startup. What do you think?"

"Why?" he would respond.

"Well, because I am tired of the corporate world, and I want to try something else," I would tell him.

"Why?"

"Because I am bored."

"Why?"

"Because I have more to give."

"Why?"

"Because it took me about three months to figure out how to do my current job, and now, I can do it in my sleep."

"Why?"

"Because it is a menial task, and I can look at the calendar next month and know what I will be doing on each day, and that is making me crazy."

This would go on and on until he would say something like: "Well, I suppose you ought to try something else. But I would be careful about the path of entrepreneurship; it's not for the faint of heart."

Yeah, no kidding, Calvin!

Through these conversations, he was answering my questions by training my brain to not rest until it came to a satisfactory conclusion that led to the truth. Often, we think the role of the mentee is to show up and have wisdom rain down on us, but in my experience, humans are pretty poor mind readers. So, when you show up to meet with your mentor, come to them with a question that needs to be examined, then listen intently.

On a real, practical level, you might be asking, *How do you even find a mentor?* Well, look in your life at people who are living in a way that you would like to live. Then simply approach them and ask them for some of their time to help you with a specific question. By doing this, the two of you can get to know each other and get a feel for what it might be like to be in a mentor-mentee relationship. If that meeting goes well, you might ask for an additional meeting to follow up or to discuss another topic. If you like the way the relationship is heading, then you can ask them to mentor you, but remember to be specific about what you want. And if you don't know what to ask for, tell them that—I bet they have a good framework for how to move forward. Finally, don't be discouraged if they turn you down; it most likely has nothing to do with you, and they are simply expressing their boundaries.

To be a good mentee, you will have the ability to:

1. **Clarify what you need.** Asking for what you need allows you and your mentor to know where to focus.

2. **Choose wisely.** Seek counsel from the right people.

3. **Underpromise and overdeliver.** On time is late, and 10 minutes early is on time.

4. **Mind the time.** If time is the most valuable resource, guard your mentor's time like an armored truck.

5. **Be invested.** Respect your mentor for the free and valuable gift they are giving you.

HOW TO BE A MENSCH

I walked into one of my favorite restaurants in Dallas, Neighborhood Services, ready to make the case for why everything in my marriage that was wrong was Angela's fault. I believed I had reams of evidence that could convince the most rational and balanced jury of this fact. At some point along the way, I had stopped being a partner in the marriage and started collecting evidence instead. I ordered a drink and waited for Jeremy to arrive, as I scrolled through my emails and Slack and responded to the metaphorical fires that had started that day.

A few moments later, Jeremy entered, ordered his drink, and asked how I was doing. We had done away with small talk years ago, so I took this as my cue to unleash my torrent of evidence. I was more intense with each sentence, knowing that Jeremy would not be easily convinced. He had known Angela and me for nearly our entire marriage, and like most people, he knew that I got the better end of the deal when Angela took my hand in marriage.

Intoxicated on the numbing effect of my first drink, I ordered a second, intent on doing my best to ignore my emotions. I waited for Jeremy to respond to my accusations. He sat back in his chair, and in his laid-back Texas drawl, he said some of the most important words I had ever heard.

"I don't know, Nick. It seems to me that if you are willing to work on a new relationship after your marriage, you might as well use that same energy to work on your current marriage."

As Flannery O'Connor said, "The truth does not change according to our ability to stomach it."[60]

Jeremy was right, and I was pissed. I wanted to win the argument, and he wanted me to win in life. *There is nothing more hostile to reality than self-deception.*

Jeremy was at that moment a mensch to me. A Yiddish and German word, *mensch* means "someone to admire and emulate."[61] Just like countless other times before, Jeremy saved me from making a self-inflicted poor decision consequence. He was able to point out my blind spots and help me see what I either refused to see or couldn't see. Unlike a mentor, who has walked the path before, a mensch is walking right beside you in a similar season of life.

Every Good Entrepreneur needs a mensch to walk with. And they also need to strive to be the kind of mensch others will want to emulate.

In order to find a good mensch, look for these attributes:

1. **Provide reality.** Be a mirror, reflecting what you see with precision, clarity, and love.
2. **Provide a relationship.** They will sit in the well with you and understand your needs.
3. **Be present.** Show up when no one else will.
4. **Not try to fix it.** They will provide a space for you to hear yourself talk. It's remarkable what we can tell ourselves.
5. **Instill confidence.** Sometimes all we need is someone to believe in us.

As you create your legacy, you'll realize, too, the power of pouring into others, both by being a mensch for them and mentoring them. You get to give back. Because as the Good Entrepreneur, you know that your success is about more than just you; one of the greatest gifts is to be able to help those around you.

END-OF-CHAPTER HOMEWORK
Create or bolster your triangle of life

Can you identify at least one person for each of these roles?

If you can't think of any names of people who are in your triangle, then your job is simple. Begin to look for people with whom to cultivate these relationships. It can take months and even years before you find the right fit; just be aware of opportunities as you develop and continue in relationships with people.

If you can identify people for these roles in your life, it's because you recognize the value in surrounding yourself with good influences. Take out your journal and write down their names, why they are in your triangle, and what you can do to enhance those relationships. Look at the five skills listed in each section below for the mentor, mentee, and mensch, and give yourself a grade of 1–10 (one being poor and 10 being excellent) for how you are performing regarding each skill.

Which skills are you excelling at (score of 8–10)?
Which skills need a little work to improve (score of 5–7)?
Which skills need a major overhaul (score of 1–4)?

Mentor skills

1. Listen.
2. Strip away everything that doesn't matter.
3. Be a professional question asker.
4. Provide perspective.
5. Tell stories.

Mentee skills

1. Clarify what you need.
2. Choose wisely.

3. Underpromise and overdeliver.
4. Mind the time.
5. Be invested.

Mensch skills

1. Provide reality.
2. Provide a relationship.
3. Be present.
4. Not try to fix it.
5. Instill confidence.

PRINCIPLE SEVEN

LIVE YOUR VALUES, EVEN WHEN NO ONE IS LOOKING

THE INVISIBLE HAND

If history has taught us anything, it is that *humans have a seemingly unlimited capacity for self-rationalization and self-delusion.* Believing that the end justifies the means, any of us can get caught up and become convinced that cutting corners is the only way to move forward.

So how do we make sure we don't become one of the many entrepreneurs who have done this?

In 1776, Adam Smith published his magnum opus, *An Inquiry into the Nature and Causes of the Wealth of Nations*, better known as *Wealth of Nations*.[62] The Scotsman collected data for 17 years, and among other things, he claimed that free trade among the members of a society inevitably leads to an outcome that is good for the society as a whole. Even though each individual pursues his own selfish gain, it can still lead to an outcome that is good for society as a whole. He noted, "It is not from the benevolence of the butcher, the brewer, or the baker that we expect our dinner, but from their regard to their own interest. We address ourselves, not to their humanity *but to their self-love* (altered for emphasis)."[63]

In other words, our own self-preservation is key to the success of our economy.

Smith is credited with creating the term *the invisible hand*, the metaphor for the unforeseen forces in the free market economy, even though it only appears one time in the book's nearly 1,000 pages.[64]

The invisible hand metaphor contains two critical ideas: "that voluntary trades in a free market produce unintended… benefits [and] these benefits are greater than those of a regulated… economy (altered for clarity and emphasis)."[65] You don't need to look beyond the laissez-faire approach that the United States has taken to see the benefits of the invisible hand. We have several hundred years of empirical evidence to prove one of the greatest economic theories humans have ever conceived.

Over 200 years later, in 1985, in *Habits of the Heart: Individualism and Commitment in American Life*, Robert Bellah examined the values of several hundred Americans.[66] He coined the term *ontological individualism*—that is, the self is the only real thing that matters in the world—Bellah concluded that for Americans in the 1980s individualism *reigned supreme*. Whether in business, marriage, or church, the "personal" needs became the main goal, just as Smith had prescribed.

You don't have to look beyond Billy McFarland, Elizabeth Holmes, Enron, Bernie Madoff, Lehman Brothers, WorldCom, Tyco, or Gordon Gecko to know that too much greed can bring ruin to both a business and a reputation. None of us nor our industries are immune to this potential fate. It takes decades to build a good reputation and minutes to lose it.

Most leaders would say, "Oh, those people aren't like me. Those people are criminals, intent on defrauding their investors. I don't have the capacity to do that."

But there are two problems with that train of thought. The first is what I stated above: Humans have a seemingly *unlimited capacity for self-rational-*

ization and self-delusion. Believing that the end justifies the means, any of us can get caught up and convinced that cutting corners is the only way to move forward. And the second is that the pressure to perform in business is often greater than the ability to stop and think about the long-term effects of our choices, particularly when individualism is the chief aim of society.

When Adam Smith wrote about "the benevolence of the butcher, the brewer, or the baker that we expect our dinner, but from their regard to their own interest,"[67] he was absolutely right. But in 1776, the butcher, the brewer, and the baker all lived in the same small village. And if the baker went to the butcher and purchased a pound of meat only to get home and find that he had received three-quarters of a pound because the butcher had fixed his scales "not to their humanity but to their self-love," you better believe that the next time the baker saw the butcher, words (and perhaps fists) would have been exchanged.

In 1776 Adam Smith couldn't have imagined that in the not-too-distant future, a new technology, called the internet, would arrive. This technology would allow people to do business with others all over the world, far beyond just their small village. Because of this technology, global and local economies would grow exponentially, the proverbial pie would be made larger, and growth would be everywhere, proving Smith's theories correct—up to a point.

With the pressure to perform so high and our capacity for corruption so great, how do we stay ethical when we may never have to look into the eyes of the person doing business with us?

With the internet in place, gone is the fear of running into the victim of your fraud on one of the few streets in the village. This physical separation in business now allows humans to act "not to their humanity but to their self-love," without ever having to confront the person on the other end of the exchange. Here we have a power imbalance.

As Good Entrepreneurs, we have the responsibility to understand these differences, build our companies accordingly, and hold other business leaders accountable. Business is never less than profits (no margin, no mission), but it should be so much more than profits. The stakeholders of any business, the employees, the investors, the customers, the vendors, and the community in which they operate are all affected by the way a business handles itself. And any leader in that business has the ability to multiply the impact they have through every decision they make, both positively and negatively.

When my dad was in prison, Angel Tree[68] volunteers would show up with gifts at my home on Christmas morning so we would have presents to open up. Why did they give their resources to us? For that matter, why does anyone do something that benefits someone else? Why does an organization like Convoy of Hope consistently show up to help when natural disasters occur?[69] What are they working toward? What is it that caused William Wilberforce to stand up against slavery in 1787 and fight for 50 years to get laws passed to abolish it in England?[70] What is it that makes us otherwise selfish beings choose to do good?

I think the answer lies in our values. When we know what we value, we act out of that. And when Good Entrepreneurs know what they value, they build their businesses out of that.

We are never more dangerous than in our own self-righteousness. This is why Soviet dissident Aleksandr Solzhenitsyn was right when he wrote from the gulag, "The line separating good and evil passes not through states, nor between classes, nor between political parties either—but right through every human heart."[71]

Even the most rational approach to business ethics is defenseless if there isn't the will to do what is right. As a Good Entrepreneur, you no longer have the option to not have an opinion on these issues. Your stakeholders, your clients, your coworkers, your customers, your investors, your community, your vendors—they're all looking to you to see what you value and how your business will reflect that. And believe it or not, you have everything you need to make the best decisions for yourself and your business if you know what you value.

STAKEHOLDERS

One of my board members invited me to join him at a CEO summit put on by Conscious Capitalism. I showed up not knowing what to expect and found myself taking 25 pages worth of notes over the course of three days. I was blown away by what the speakers were saying. The idea behind Conscious Capitalism is best described by R. Edward Freedman when he said, "We need red blood cells to live (the same way a business needs profits to live), but the purpose of life is more than to make red blood cells (the same way the purpose of business is more than simply to generate profits)."[72]

The weekend helped me see that recognizing and valuing everyone who is affected by your business is essential to the success of the Good Entrepreneur.

Providing a paycheck to your employee puts food in their (and their dependents') mouths and shelter over their heads, literally providing the first two levels of Maslow's hierarchy of needs.[73] Knowing that makes being able to pay someone else one of the highest honors for an entrepreneur. It can also make it one of the most gut-wrenching experiences. It makes the stakes higher for any leader. Knowing you have to find a way to make payroll happen when you don't have the money is a difficult challenge that I think almost every entrepreneur will face. But when you've created a company that values its employees and the people in their lives, you learn to rise to the occasion and figure it out.

Beyond employees, providing for the other stakeholders is key to any successful business. By providing a return to your investors, they will be more enthusiastic to provide capital the next time you ask. By paying vendors fairly and on time, you will help their businesses thrive so they can continue to grow. By actively participating in the communities in which you operate, you're investing in their long-term success and ensuring that those not directly involved with your business still benefit from your success.

Finally, by providing a product that customers receive value from and want to buy more of, you're creating consistent and long-term revenue that powers the entire organization.

Simply put, when the five stakeholders—employees, customers, investors, partners, and communities—are all properly aligned, it is almost impossible to not be successful as a business, both financially and beyond.

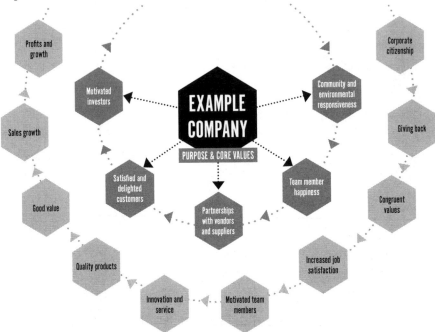

If this process seems too Pollyanna-ish, you should know that it is a system that has been in place at some of the most beloved companies in America, such as Costco, The Container Store, Whole Foods, Southwest Airlines, Alphabet, Starbucks, and many more. These companies are providing higher financial returns while proving that is not their only purpose. In fact, in a study of 18 publicly traded Conscious Capitalist organizations, these companies outperformed the S&P 500 by 10.5 times.[74]

VALUES, VISION, AND PURPOSE

I walked out of that weekend a changed entrepreneur. From there, I immediately began to sketch out the culture that I wanted to create at RISE by defining our purpose, vision, and values.

When I started RISE, I had plans to run it for many decades to come. As such, I was hopeful that I would have employees who would be along with me for the full ride and even beyond. However, I knew from previous experience that one of the hardest things about starting a business is knowing that the people who start with you will often not be the people who end with you.

Why *do* I say all of this? To remind you (and me) that Good Entrepreneurs value their employees by investing in them. Employees spend more waking hours at work than they do almost anywhere else. Imagine if the culture you created welcomed them, got to know them, and helped them become a better version of themselves. Instead of walking into an environment where they felt threatened and triggered, shrinking under the pressure, unable to grow in their role and life, they'd walk into an environment that nurtured, challenged, and helped them thrive. As Good Entrepreneurs, you have the potential to create an environment that does just that.

I had been burned in the past by enough bosses who only cared about their "self-love," and I wanted to be different. So, I wrote down that the purpose of RISE was to take care of its employees.

Now, this didn't mean that they got a free ride, nor did it mean that we were the best employer ever. But it did mean that we worked every day to build long-term success so that our stakeholders would want to reward us, and we could in turn continue our conscious commitment to thinking beyond profits and taking care of our people. Because when you value taking care of your employees, the profits will take care of themselves.

Next, I took out my pen and wrote our vision:

"To give our members the most valuable commodity in the world: time."

Yes, we were providing access to private planes (nearly 75% of our members had never flown private before), but I knew that "wow" factor would wear off with enough use. We would need staying power if we wanted decades of success. This vision gave us that. Everything we did was about giving time back to our members, and valuing this vision paid off in spades. We all knew what was most important to the company, and we all valued it in everything we did. We didn't want to waste our members' time. I demanded that our technology be able to book a flight in less than ten seconds, phones were to be answered within two rings, cars were waiting planeside, and the coffee bar was to be accessible on the way out the door to the plane. In short, everything we did was about saving time because that was what we valued for our members.

Every time a member flew on RISE, we aimed to give them three hours back in their day. We saved our members an hour and a half on the front end between parking, checking in, waiting in line, going through TSA, boarding the plane, collecting their bags, picking up their rental car, and more. And then we saved them an hour and a half on the back end between dropping off the rental car, and, once again, checking their bags, going through TSA, and waiting to board, only to get crammed in like a herd of cattle. And because of that, we aimed to give our members a 10 times better experience than flying commercial at a 10th of the cost of chartering or owning their own private plane.

All of those may seem like minute details of the business, but to us, they were so much more. These actions were borne out of the purpose and vision that we valued.

In the book *Start with Why: How Great Leaders Inspire Everyone to Take Action*,[75] Simon Sinek writes, "Very few people or companies can clearly articulate *why* they do *what* they do. By *why* I mean your purpose, cause or belief—*why* does your company exist? *Why* do you get out of bed every morning? And *why* should anyone care? (Altered for emphasis.)" We now had our why. We existed to take care of our employees so they could give time back to our members.

I had an idea of what our values should be, but I knew that if I came up with them in a vacuum, they would not be owned by the rest of the team. So, we gathered together and had a discussion about what we wanted our values to be. We discussed how our *values* ultimately determined our *culture*. So, the question we were really addressing was what type of environment we could create that would make them so proud that they would want to recruit their friends to come work for us.

We wrote down every value that the team liked and discussed why they thought them important, then we grouped the values into categories, finally coming up with the values that we wanted. The following became the values that created the culture of RISE:

- Love: We believe in demonstrating love in all that we do, through respect and selflessness.
- Selfless leadership: We're givers. People who are too me-centered do not fit at RISE.
- Excellence: We do great things with the gifts that have been given to us.
- Courage: It is not always comfortable being courageous, but it is vital to the success of RISE.
- Integrity: Be honest in all things. Do what you say even though it may cost you.
- Fun: By refusing to take ourselves too seriously, we are more energized and driven.

THE FUTURE IS BRIGHT

Being that we were a startup and hadn't yet seen the success that I knew was to come, we had to make decisions based on reality, not dreams. As such, we hired mainly millennials to be forward-facing to our members because they were fresh out of college and their salary expectations were within my budget. I was warned time and again about how this generation would not make good employees and that we were going to suffer the consequences. And to be honest, I even believed it.

Which is why here, I must say this:

Dear millennials, I was wrong about you. Please forgive me.

The word *millennial* elicits a response within most of us these days. This generation, defined as anyone born between 1980 and 1995, was raised by doting baby boomers who told them constantly how special they were. They have a room full of participation trophies and are often known for being hard to manage.[76] They are also redefining the work world in real time, and I think it's for the better.

Given that millennials make up the majority of the workers in the United States, I think we should all be optimistic about our future. New businesses, new technologies, and new ideas are sprouting up from a generation that isn't deterred by the word *no*.

These young people reject institutional rules with righteous indignation. As a result, financial and social goals are becoming linked; the line is becoming blurred more and more every day. Today's young, socially motivated generation doesn't respect the walls between government, nonprofits, and business; in fact, they ask why the walls exist at all.

Working side by side with this generation at RISE, my perception changed, and my eyes were opened to their potential. Now I describe millennials as determined, transparent, and authentic.

WE ARE HERE TO HELP

That year at the Conscious Capitalism CEO summit in Austin, Texas, I had the opportunity to hear Kristen Hadeed speak.[77] She's a force to be reckoned with, a dynamic speaker, and a successful entrepreneur with seemingly interminable energy. Kristen is the founder of Student Maid, a cleaning service dedicated to empowering the rising generation of leaders and the author of the book *Permission to Screw Up*.[78]

She started her talk with a question: "How do you get millennials to clean toilets?" She then proceeded to tell the story of how she built a business that is making money based on having a helper's heart.

She wanted a pair of jeans, and as a poor college student, she didn't have the money to buy them. She appealed to her parents, who wouldn't give her the money, and they told her to get a job.

She needed something flexible that would work around her demanding schedule, something that would allow her to be her own boss. So, Kristen put an ad on Craigslist to clean houses. One house turned to two, and two houses turned to three, and soon she found herself needing help. So, she did what an entrepreneur would do—she hired other students to help.

"I found that our clients grew attached to our students. We were being invited to Thanksgiving dinners and being asked to house-sit and pet-sit.

They trusted us. So, we decided to offer it all, whether it's cleaning, organizing, dog walking, or another chore needing attention. Our theme was 'We are here to help.'"

"We are here to help." A concept that is lost in a narcissistic society but embraced by an entire generation seeking authenticity.

I spent a lot of time thinking about how to grow a culture that is meaningful, challenging, and fulfilling to this generation. I instituted a weekly all-hands team meeting so we could discuss situations that had arisen over the previous week in which we had the opportunity to make decisions based on the RISE values, vision, and purpose. These ideals were much more than trite slogans to put up on our walls and later be ignored. They were the keys to our success and the differentiators that ensured our success, and I focused on reinforcing them during these meetings.

Brené Brown says, "If you put shame in a petri dish, it needs three things to grow exponentially: secrecy, silence, and judgment. If you put the same amount of shame in a petri dish and douse it with empathy, it can't survive."[79] We would end those Monday meetings with an opportunity to be transparent and empathetic with the rest of the company.

"Tell Nick something he doesn't want to know" is a game we often played. Why? Because it proved that we all make bad decisions. It built trust. It provided a great opportunity for us to build community, but more importantly, it allowed us to give immediate feedback. We were separating shame from guilt. *Shame says, "I am bad," Guilt says, "I did something bad." Guilt is "I am sorry I made that bad choice." Shame is "I am sorry I am bad." Two drastically different thoughts.*

One of the worst confessions I received was from one of our millennial employees. They shared that they returned a brand-new Mercedes Benz to Hertz Car Rental, only realizing their poor decision when our member landed and had no car to drive home.

I used these opportunities to repeat another value over and over: "The goal is not to be perfect; the goal is to be a 1% better version of yourself tomorrow than you were today. Ingest and learn from your decisions, share them liberally so that your colleagues won't have the same consequences, and we can all look forward to better versions of ourselves."

We sometimes *make* bad decisions—we *are not* bad decisions.

We removed secrecy, silence, and judgment, and we thrived.

I am pleasantly surprised to tell you that most aspects of the millennial stereotype are not consistent with my experience. I have found the opposite of what I'd expected in my preconceived ignorance. Even when these employees made a poor decision, they quickly owned it and made it right.

This is our future, and our future is bright. Why? Because millennials force us *to live* our values. They are Good Entrepreneurs in the making.

They are going to better this world, and I'm glad that I'm here to witness it.

100 YEARS FROM NOW

In his book, *The Good Ancestor: How to Think Long Term in a Short-Term World*, the philosopher Roman Krznaric advises, "At the very least, when you aim to think 'long term,' take a deep breath and think 'a hundred years and more.'"[80] This is a good litmus test for whatever it is you're working on. One hundred years from now, will anyone be talking about the work you have done? The influence you had? The character that set you apart? Defining and living by your values will help ensure that a hundred years from now, someone somewhere will remember you not just for what you did but how you lived.

As an example, Krzanric discusses Jonas Salk, who cured polio in 1953, saving millions of lives, but he refused to patent his cure or make money from it. We live in a world in which we focus on the next quarter, next election, or timing of markets, hardly ever considering if we will have influence after we are gone. Krzanric concludes, "We rarely stop to consider whether we're being good ancestors … but the future depends on it."

THE FUTURE DEPENDS ON IT

As you continue on your own path toward becoming a Good Entrepreneur, you have two choices. You can either sit back, wait for the challenges to arise, and then decide how to deal with them, or you can set out laser focused on your values, vision, and purpose from the very beginning. Knowing what you want and value from the start is a lot easier than trying to figure it out or make it up as you go.

So, if you have determined what you value in your life, in your work, or for your organization, write it down. Disseminate and bring it into your daily routine. Start living it out. Remember that in marketing it is said that it takes the average person around seven times to hear something before they truly remember it.[81] Talk about your values. Make them a regular part of the conversation with your team, your family, your coworkers, or whoever is in your sphere of influence. Make them something people will remember.

And if you haven't yet defined what it is you value, there is no time like the present. Carve out some quiet time by yourself, read the obituary that you created, remember the people who influenced you, recall the stories of leaders and organizations that made you proud, and start to create your own framework to live by. Be intentional about this process. Don't wait for an opportunity to react. Creating this framework in your business and personal life will do wonders to move your life from chaos to order. It will give you your own values to live by as a Good Entrepreneur as you continue on your journey.

END-OF-CHAPTER HOMEWORK
CREATE OR REVIEW YOUR PURPOSE, VISION, AND VALUE STATEMENTS.

What is a purpose statement?

An effective vision statement expresses the desired state in an inspirational way, representing the long view and ideal outcome. It is not complicated, and its purpose is to create inspiration and to define the path to success for the employees.

Examples from different businesses:

Exists to take care of its employees (RISE—airline)

The American Cancer Society's mission is to save lives, celebrate lives, and lead the fight for a world without cancer.

(American Cancer Society)[82]

Empower people through great software anytime, anyplace, and on any device (Microsoft)[83]

To make people happy (Disney)[84]

To bring inspiration and innovation to every athlete* in the world.

*If you have a body, you are an athlete. (Nike)[85]

What is your purpose statement?

_____

What is a vision statement?

A vision statement clarifies why the organization exists and how it is unique. It embodies its values and goals.

It answers:

What do we do?

Purpose—to define an organization's reason for existence, beliefs, and approach in a way that motivates alignment throughout the organization. It is more action based than a vision statement so that employees can easily internalize it on a daily basis.

Examples include:

To give our members the most valuable commodity in the world: time. (RISE)

To accelerate the world's transition to sustainable energy. (Tesla)[86]

Spread ideas. (TED)[87]

We aim to be Earth's most customer centric company. Our mission is to continually raise the bar of the customer experience by using the internet and technology to help consumers find, discover and buy anything, and empower businesses and content creators to maximise their success. (Amazon)[88]

"Our mission is to make Target the preferred shopping destination for our guests by delivering outstanding value, continuous innovation and an exceptional guest experience by consistently fulfilling our Expect More. Pay Less.® brand promise. (Target)[89]

What is your mission statement?
_____

What are values?
Values describe how we intend to operate on a day-to-day basis as we pursue our vision and mission.

Values are exhibited in behaviors and might include:

- how we want to be treated,
- how we want to treat others, and
- lines that we will and will not cross.

Examples of values and their expected behaviors

- Love: We believe in demonstrating love in all that we do, through respect and selflessness.
- Selfless leadership: We're givers. People who are too me-centered do not fit at RISE.
- Excellence: We do great things with the gifts that have been given to us.
- Courage: It is not always comfortable being courageous, but it is vital to the success of RISE.
- Integrity: Be honest in all things. Do what you say even though it may cost you.
- Fun: By refusing to take ourselves too seriously, we are more energized and driven.

What are your core values and their expected behaviors?

Value: _____

Expected behaviors

Value: _____

Expected behaviors

Value: _____

Expected behaviors

Value: _____

Expected behaviors

Value: _____

Expected behaviors

PRINCIPLE EIGHT

ESCHEW THE GOOD FOR THE BEST

IT GETS EASIER, BUT IT NEVER GETS EASY

In my experience, the majority of publicly available information about entrepreneurship only tells a small portion of the story. Social media, keynote addresses, and television shows put forth the consumable and sexy stories that are designed to draw clicks and views. There is nothing wrong with this take as long as you know that the majority of an entrepreneur's work is a long, hard slog of seemingly never-ending problem-solving. This chapter outlines the brass tacks and the unsexy side of entrepreneurship that is necessary for success on that journey.

Part of that journey, as simple as it sounds, is just making your business work—by learning to say no. Like when looking at the menu at The Cheesecake Factory, you will have seemingly infinite options on how to deploy your resources. Your inner critic, employees, investors, vendors, and customers will all give you unsolicited advice, and your job is to know how to filter through the noise to focus on what matters. It is helpful to strip away all that is unnecessary by asking yourself if your decision helps support any of these foundations of any business:

1. Cash is king.
2. Solve a problem.
3. See around the corner.
4. Find people better than you and get out of their way.
5. Just keep going.

These principles propelled my path in business. And without them, I wouldn't have stayed afloat for long.

CASH IS KING

In the book *The One Thing* by Gary Keller with Jay Pappasan, the authors encourage readers to ask this pertinent question: "What's the *one thing* I can do such that by doing it everything else will be easier or unnecessary? (Altered for emphasis.)"[90]

This question is important for every day of our lives, but it is more important at the beginning of the journey of any Good Entrepreneur. It has the ability to strip away all that is unnecessary in order to serve the greater purpose.

So, what is the first thing to focus on as a Good Entrepreneur? Cash. Cash is like oxygen, if you run out of it, your business is dead. Without cash, your vision, values, and purpose won't matter. Taking care of your stakeholders won't matter. You won't have much to worry about because you won't have a business.

That's why you have to find a way to marry meaning with profit in your work. You have to find a way to sell your product or service at a price that the public is willing to pay. All business, at its core, is one person creating a mutually beneficial relationship with the other person. And the price of the product is determined by what your customer is willing to pay for it.

So, the first step of a clear path is to find out who your customer is. You can have a really cool widget, but if no one wants to use it, you don't have a business. If you can get into your market, listen carefully to your audience, and help your customers articulate to you what they really want, you can build a product that is truly for them. You can create a relationship between your business and your customers that is mutually beneficial. And you can start turning profit with a purpose.

One of the quickest ways to generate additional cash is to start charging more money for your product or service. It may seem counterintuitive to raise prices as you are trying to grow your market share, but companies are often *too hungry to eat*. They don't charge enough to become profitable, and it begins a nasty cycle that is hard to escape. Why not charge more and test what the market is willing to pay from the very beginning? If they are willing to pay more, then you are able to manage your cash more easily and remove one of the barriers to success. If they aren't willing to pay more, then your product may not be as good as you think, and it is much better to find that out sooner than later.

Controlling your costs is the second way that you can manage your cash. Fancy offices and over-the-top perks are necessary in some markets to recruit in-demand employees, but in most cases, those perks are often overkill, and the juice is not worth the squeeze. Until you have found your footing and have begun to optimize your business, do not expose it to unnecessary costs. There will come a time in the future when you can reap your rewards, but until that time comes, it is necessary to live on a budget, making sure the overwhelming majority of your cash goes *directly* to enhancing your product or service.

As an example, when we built the first version of our software for RISE, I told the developers I had three criteria: (1) It had to be beautiful, (2) it had to let our members book their flights in 10 seconds or less, and (3) it had to be able to charge credit cards on a recurring basis. There were countless requests for additional bells and whistles that I turned down because they didn't serve these criteria. The software developers and employees meant well, but they didn't have the same responsibility as I did. As a Good Entrepreneur, it is important to become comfortable with making other people uncomfortable in order to serve the values, vision, and purpose of your company.

Frequently, businesses are unable to be cash flow positive from the beginning, and a capital infusion is necessary to get started. If you don't have the funds to bridge the gap between an idea and generating cash, you will need to look for outside capital from investors. But at some point in the future, you are going to need to be profitable in order to pay them back, so it always comes back to making your business work by generating cash.

One of the worst places to be as an entrepreneur is in the season of perpetually raising money. Until you are generating a profit, investors are subsidizing your product, not letting the market determine its true value. Additionally, for most entrepreneurs raising money is hard, and it takes a toll on you emotionally. I know a lot of people who have raised money for their companies, but I have yet to come across one who would describe the process as enjoyable.

The upside of raising money is that it validates your idea. I have a friend who is a billionaire, and he needed to raise 100 million dollars for a business. I asked him why he didn't just use his own money. He looked at me, chuckled a little bit, and said, "Nick, almost everyone around me has something to gain by keeping me happy, so they are likely to tell me that my ideas are great ideas. So, I like to raise money, because most humans love money more than anything else, and only after they wire me their money do I know that they really believe in my idea." Talk about a situation tailor made for a mensch.

There are plenty of reasons that raising money may be the right path for you, but be very wise with regard to the amount of money you raise, knowing that the bill will come due in the future.

SOLVE A PROBLEM

Becoming an entrepreneur is just taking something that annoyed you and spending most waking moments thinking about it.

My freshman year of college, we often stayed up way too late. And because we wanted to sleep more than we wanted breakfast, we hit the snooze button until the very last minute. We perfected the getting-ready part, moving from the bed to walking out the door in only a few minutes.

The only problem? We couldn't find a way to make it to the cafeteria for breakfast. And because most college freshmen value sleep above all else, most of our friends had the same dilemma.

Every Good Entrepreneur does one thing well: solving problems. And they are willing to sacrifice their own comfort to do so. In this case, my roommate Mark (the same Mark that almost died with me in Colorado) and I decided to solve the breakfast problem by opening an all-you-can-eat pancake restaurant in our dorm room. For three dollars, you could get one pancake, but for seven dollars, you could get all you can eat. (Pro tip: we made the pancakes large and very thick so almost no one could eat more than two.) We went to Walmart and bought a flat top skillet, a spatula, and a family-size box of generic pancake mix. Then, we advertised throughout the dorm.

The next morning, we had a line out the door for breakfast. In one day, we were counting cash while flipping pancakes. We had satisfied customers, the rest of the freshmen were fed, and we were banking money for our weekend dates. It was a problem solved, until our dorm manager shut us down for running a restaurant out of our room. Turned out, that was against the rules.

That experience taught me two things. The first was that if I was experiencing a problem, chances are somebody else was experiencing the same one. Mark and I weren't the only hungry freshmen sleeping in every day. It was an issue for most of the people in our dorm, so much so that people were willing to pay for a solution. The second thing I learned was that being an entrepreneur was exhilarating. It provided an identity for me. It gave me a chance to be the creative, fun leader who people looked up to. And I liked it. It felt natural—like home.

The pancake business in my dorm room was the first of my entrepreneurial ventures. I have been fortunate to be part of several teams that have built companies from almost nothing into successful enterprises. We've created entirely new categories of businesses, provided jobs, given excellent returns to our investors, and even saved lives by applying technology to the world of oncology in one of these businesses. There were hundreds of days and sleepless nights when we didn't know if we would ever find success on any level. We took incredible risks with our money, relationships, and any other resources we could leverage. And the risks paid off because, at the root of all our businesses, we were trying to solve problems. That was always a part of our path.

Every Good Entrepreneur should always be asking, What problem am I trying to solve? Making that a clear part of your path to business will ensure that your business is always relevant. Why? Because it's providing a much-needed solution to a tension or pain point for your customers.

The entrepreneurial journey is in some ways a contract that you make with yourself to be unsatisfied until you solve a problem. My advice is to make sure the problem you pick is a big one in order to reap a large return on your investment.

SEE AROUND THE CORNER

I hear CEOs talk about how lonely it is at the top, and I agree. The weight of the world is sitting on the shoulders of the CEO, and often, they bear that weight alone. They are the tip of the spear—powerful yet alone.

The CEO is typically the only person in the whole organization who has a view into all the key aspects of the business. They confer with the sales and marketing leaders in order to know the outlook for sales or how much cash they are going to generate. Then they meet with the head of operations to see how they are doing on executing on the promises delivered to the customer and what it costs to do so. Then the head of finance provides an outlook of how much cash will be left over and advises what to do with it. The CEO's privileged position gives them access to all the different information necessary to make the hard decisions.

At the beginning of any venture, the entrepreneur often holds all of these positions because they are the only employee. This season is great training for understanding all the aspects of the business and how a decision in one part of the business affects the others.

The head of sales may want to hire more sales executives in order to hit their aggressive sales goals, but the head of finance just delivered the news that one of their largest clients is consistently paying their invoices late, tightening cash flow and not allowing the business to make the investment at that time. It is the CEO who needs to make the next decision. The CEO has to be able to communicate to finance and sales what is best for the business. They have to see both what is happening now and what's ahead.

In other words, the CEO has to be able to see around the corner. To see around the corner is to synthesize information from outside of the organization and inside the organization. It's to predict what the future will bring and align the company to take advantage of that future. It's an important part of defining a clear path. Because if you want to follow a clear path as a Good Entrepreneur, you have to be able to see every twist and turn along the way.

As a Good Entrepreneur, you have to be able to see truth, ingest it, and articulate it, even if it's a harsh reality to face.

Any time I have a new idea, I ask a couple of friends—my mensches—to grab drinks or dinner. There, I pitch them my idea and gauge their reactions. Most of my ideas never get past this stage. These are close friends who aren't afraid to tell me when my ideas stink. They're not afraid to help me see around the corner, for better or for worse.

I take the few ideas that make it out of that gauntlet of scrutiny and start to socialize them with a larger group of people. I try to gauge the industry expertise of this second group. I am not a believer that you need to be an expert in a field to be successful. In fact, sometimes expertise can be a problem. It tempts you to accept what has always been as opposed to finding a new way. But leaning into the voices of experts at different points in the path can be helpful.

In the case of RISE, I knew that I couldn't fly the planes, but I also knew I could hire pilots to do that. So, I started telling friends about my idea, and they did what they always do if they like my idea: they offered to find a way to help. When your idea is good, people line up to help you on your journey, sensing an opportunity to leave a legacy for themselves. Before long, I was in touch with a couple of pilots, and a couple of owners of planes, and a couple of owners of the management companies of planes.

I would have coffee, lunch, dinner, or drinks with these people—whatever it took to get to the expertise I needed to help me see around the corner. This part of the path was exhausting, but it was pure fun for me.

What I learned during those exploratory meetings was that the average private plane in America is woefully underutilized. These multimillion-dollar planes sit around in hangars, waiting to be used for much of the time.

Knowing this, I picked up the phone to call a dozen plane management companies in Texas. I introduced myself and pitched them my idea. And you know what happened? Almost every single one of them told me I was crazy. "No one from outside the industry could be successful; it was too complicated," they would explain. But eventually a couple operators met with me, thinking I might be the solution to their problem of plateaued growth.

Using existing planes and operators was the linchpin to our business because we were creating a two-sided marketplace. At this time, Uber and Lyft were growing rapidly, and they were able to do so because they were able to use assets owned by other people. At RISE, I called this "OPP," as in "Other People's Planes." By not owning the planes ourselves, we could grow more rapidly. I knew that because I was always looking around the corner. If we tried to buy the planes, we would need tens of millions of dollars now and hundreds of millions later, if my growth projections panned out.

Every Good Entrepreneur needs to look ahead. They need to see around the corner of the path they're on so they can not only predict and project growth but see and avoid failure as well.

FIND PEOPLE BETTER THAN YOU AND GET OUT OF THEIR WAY

In my case, one of the questions that continually came up was, How am I going to get planes in the air? It was a valid question for my business, and I didn't know the answer. Even though I had the idea in my head, I needed to get both the Federal Aviation Administration (FAA), which regulates air safety, and the Department of Transportation (DOT), which regulates consumer protection, to agree with me.

That wouldn't be that hard, right? Well, I was about to run smack dab into the messy middle of federal-government bureaucracy. I just had no idea what that task would entail.

The key to making the whole business model work was OPP, but because it had never been done before, we had to make the case for it. We researched the law, created a case for allowing us to provide air travel this way, and presented it in writing. Being new to this industry, I relied heavily on the experts and attorneys to help with this step.

But I quickly figured out that, in spite of paying them handsomely, my experts were not versed in the way of entrepreneurship, and our expectations were vastly different. I had been promised that their exorbitant fees were worth it because "they knew people who could expedite the process." Turned out, that was code for "I did two decades of hellish work on the inside so I could get out and sell my access to the highest bidder." Regardless, I just held my nose and paid the fees.

After we submitted the request, we didn't hear anything. Days turned to weeks, and weeks turned to months. Finally, I was exasperated and demanded some progress. So, I asked for a meeting with the powers that be. At first, I was met with a rejection. "That is not how this works," I was told. But after I reminded them that they promised me access and that their prescribed course of action wasn't working for me, they called their former friends and scheduled a meeting.

When we arrived at the DOT building in Washington, DC, we were ushered into an interior meeting room with no windows and seating for about 20 people. My team sat on one side of the table, anxiously awaiting the arrival of someone from the DOT so we could plead our case. The first group arrived, and a couple of employees scurried to the end of the table. I was then caught by surprise when more people joined us. I leaned toward my attorney and asked why so many people would attend this meeting about my little startup.

I knew walking into this meeting that there was a very asymmetric risk and reward system with regulators. If they agree to something new and something bad happens, they could lose their careers. But if something good happens, they don't even get a reward. If you were faced with big punishment for one outcome and no reward for the other, how would you respond?

My attorney leaned in without making eye contact and said, "It's not every day that someone who has no experience in airlines shows up at the DOT to ask for permission to start one. You are like the two-headed snake at the state fair! Everyone wants to see it, but they have no idea why."

I was distraught, confused, and running out of cash while waiting for the wheels of bureaucracy to turn. And then, to add insult to injury, apparently, I was the laughingstock of this whole meeting and paying $800 per hour to boot. With that revelation, my attorney opened the meeting with introductions all around.

If there is one thing that I know how to do, it's read a room. I have a keen ability to analyze my audience and edit my presentation in real time to address their specific skepticisms. There are two rules to public speaking that I try to never forget. First, connect with the audience and empathize with their needs. And second, entertain them. This is what really gets them invested.

In that sterile boardroom that day, it was my time to shine.

I told them my story. How I had spent two million miles packed in like a sardine on commercial flights. How I had endured delays, rerouting, rude flight attendants, huge change fees, and every other frustration any veteran traveler would know well. How I had a history of coming into industries that I had no experience in, finding some fundamental flaws that had not been fixed, and helping them build businesses designed to address the problem while making money. How I saw the same inefficiencies in air travel. How the gap between private air travel and legacy air carriers was vast and needed to be closed. How I believed that RISE was built to do just that.

They peppered us with questions about how we proposed to deal with specific regulations, and we responded with our well-thought-out arguments. I had no desire to start RISE only to get it shut down in our first few months of flying; I needed this to last for decades. It was being built to last, with no shortcuts and no gray area. Lives and livelihoods were at stake.

I see so many entrepreneurs looking for a shooting star—something to grow quickly and make them money before moving on to something else. I, too, was once like that, but I knew how quickly the burn fizzled. So, I was determined to build something to last, and taking a shortcut or finding a loophole would not cut it for me.

I do not hide my frustrations well. I am a horrible liar, which turned out to be a really good characteristic in situations like that one. Why? Because all those people I was trying to get involved on the path to RISE with me believed me. They looked into my eyes, and by the time the 90-minute meeting was over, even the top bureaucrat was with me.

"We want you to be successful," he said. "We know that competition brings a better experience for everyone, and we desperately want it, but because of the high cost of entry, you don't see many new entrants. It will be a tough road for you, but we will do what we can to help. It is so frustrating to get letters about consumers' negative experiences, and because of the lobbying power of the airlines, our hands are tied, and we can't effect much change."

I was dumbfounded. Ninety minutes earlier, I had thought this trip was a waste of money, and now we were walking away with a victory. Even our attorneys were surprised about the outcome of the meeting.

The point of this story? Good Entrepreneurs know that part of the path is getting other people involved. They know that the path can't be walked or won alone. And because of that, they're prepared not only to get other people involved but to get the right people involved. The people who will help you keep moving down the path toward your goal.

JUST KEEP GOING

Even as you learn to master all these principles and walk the clear path you've set before you, there will be factors beyond your control. Some will be peaks—the height of excitement, success, and achievement. And others?

They'll be valleys—the moments that can bring you to your knees. The path of the Good Entrepreneur is filled with both.

After I flew home from Washington D.C., I expected everything to work out easily. I had been assured by all those who knew—those who had been in the industry for decades—that it would all work out in the end. With that assurance, I moved forward, hiring employees, painting planes, setting up new offices, and finding new members. I was ready to go, tired of sitting on the sidelines and itching to start flying.

Unfortunately, the DOT had other plans. Little did I know that their promise, "We will do what we can to help," meant something completely different to me than it did my new friends in Washington. Their way wasn't fast enough for me. They would reach out periodically for additional information, which we would submit quickly. Then they would take weeks or even months to respond with additional questions. I was burning the candle at both ends, but they were in no hurry.

To make matters worse, all of this back-and-forth was done via a public website in which anybody could search and see an application. I was nervous that a competitor was going to find our application, see our business plans, steal them from us, and move forward before we even got off the ground. To say this was a valley in my path would be an understatement.

One week turned to one month. One month turned to two. The process seemed to never end. I had started on top of the world, but at this point, I was questioning all of my assumptions. The cash that we had raised to support growth was now being used just to survive.

At about month five, my frustration really started to grow. I began to get nervous that this valley was the end of the path. I was not taking a salary at this time—a commitment I had made to myself and my investors until we started flying. Now, I had to reach out to mentors and mensches to ask if they would do the same, knowing that my personal cash situation was mimicking that of my business. Each person I spoke with reminded me of my commitment and that my word was more important than my comfort. After all, we had no revenue coming in, so an additional expense made little sense.

During this time, I met a new liaison at the DOT named Sarah (not her real name). Sarah was a lower-level bureaucrat whose job was to monitor our application, ask for any additional information, and keep us abreast of the timeline. Unfortunately for me, Sarah was under stringent rules about what she could and could not share with me. And unfortunately for her, I was not one to take no for an answer.

Just as I was calling Sarah on repeat, my investors and members who had signed up with us were regularly calling me wondering when they could fly. And if they weren't calling, my worried employees were peppering me with their own questions. Although I told them what I knew, what I knew wasn't much. With each week that went by, my credibility evaporated more and more. The valley got deeper.

Soon, my wife, Angela, was frustrated too. Her frustrations around finances, my workaholism, and my continued increase in drinking were all legitimate. We had reached a pivotal point in the path.

I was stuck in a paradox. On the outside, it looked like I was at a peak. My face was being printed in magazines and newspapers. I was being invited to all the parties. But below the surface, the valley was real. My cash was draining by the day. My chief fear was that we would run out of cash while waiting for approval, never launch RISE, lose all our investors' money, and end up with a dozen lawsuits.

At the root was the fear that, somehow, I'd end up in the same position as my father. So, every time an angry investor would call wanting answers, I would go to a dark place. To be clear, I wasn't doing anything illegal. On the contrary, I instructed my attorneys to help me make every decision in a conservative manner, never even giving the impression of taking shortcuts. But in the end, none of that matters in the court of public opinion when people lose money.

My emotions were all over the place. I was riding the peak with the never-ending invitations to events and sitting down in the valley each week when Sarah told me it wasn't going to be my week. It felt like my entire identity was on the line. And there, the valley got darker. I didn't have a healthy mechanism to share my fears. Instead, I chose to drown my pain in alcohol and work. I would lash out at my employees, my family, and my friends. I knew I was being a jerk, but I didn't care. My kingdom was crumbling, and I thrashed about as it did, causing collateral damage with every move. On the outside, not getting approval to fly meant we would never fly, which was a terrible situation. But on the inside, I was dying under the fear that I was going to be a failure—that my path was going to end in this valley.

After receiving the latest rejection from Sarah, I went into my bedroom and sat on my bed. Angela followed me and sat by my side, asking me what was happening. With tears streaming down my cheeks and my body shaking, I finally confessed out loud what had been echoing in my head.

I didn't know how this was going to turn out.

Outwardly, I put on a show of confidence, but on my bed that day, I broke down and shared all my fears. Once the fears were spoken into the ether, Angela held me and spoke words of affirmation to me. She didn't tell me that I was going to be successful but rather that she would always be there by my side. I desperately wanted her words to be true, but I didn't believe they were. I thought my worth was set in my ability to be successful. I thought that was all there was to my path.

In *The Hard Thing About Hard Things: Building a Business When There Are No Easy Answers*, Ben Horowitz tells the following story about his time as a CEO:

> At times like this, it's important to understand that nearly every company goes through life-threatening moments. My partner at Andreessen Horowitz, Scott Weiss, relayed that it's so common that there is an acronym for it, WFIO, which stands for 'We're F**ked, It's Over.' (It's pronounced 'whiff-ee-yo.') As he describes it, every company goes through at least two and up to five of these episodes (although I'm pretty sure that I went through at least a dozen at Opsware). In all cases, WFIOs feel much worse than they are—especially for the CEO.[91]

I think any Good Entrepreneur can relate because every journey contains peaks and valleys. We can't have one without the other. And if we want to keep walking the path toward success, we have to be willing to lean into and learn from both.

That day, I was smack dab in the middle of my first WFIO moment. What I wanted more than anything else in the world was to survive it so I would have the privilege of facing the next one that came my way.

Because these moments—these deep and dark valleys—are part of the process. They're part of the path. And any Good Entrepreneur who has a clear path knows they're just moments. They will pass and give way to a new peak. But we won't know unless we keep going.

Unless we keep following our clear path.

END-OF-CHAPTER HOMEWORK
HOW CLEAR IS YOUR PATH?

For this exercise, take out your journal and write down the five principles from the beginning of the chapter:

- Cash is king.
- Solve a problem.
- See around the corner.
- Get others on board.
- Just keep going.

Now, for each principle, give yourself a score from 1–10 based on how you are doing in that area (One being the worst and 10 being the best). If you are running low on cash and you are consistently worried about payroll, you are much closer to a one than a 10. If you have a product, but no one is using it, does it really solve a problem? What are your 10-year, five-year, one-year, and six-month strategic plans for your business? Are you leaning on others to help and not trying to be a lone wolf? Take your time, and be honest in your evaluation.

Once you have scored each principle, rank them from lowest to highest. You now have the priorities for your business figured out. Now is the time to attack each one in order (starting with the lowest score and working toward the highest score).

- What is the takeaway from your example?
- What action will you take this week to increase your score?
- Who do you need to ask for help?

Do this exercise once a month, and keep track of your scores in a spreadsheet so you keep a history of them, making it easier to see patterns in your business. I guarantee if you excel at these principles, your will be well on your way to success. If a distraction arises that doesn't support one of these four principles, put it on the back burner until you have better stability.

PRINCIPLE NINE

STAY SCRAPPY TO SURVIVE

SURVIVAL MODE

My friend Ezra is a former professional poker player, a successful venture capitalist, and the kind of guy who never minces his words. He wrote the following truth in a blog not too long ago: "There is a growing cancer in many emerging startup ecosystems: a glut of self-congratulatory awards shows and banquets that honor both local advocates of entrepreneurship as well as early-stage startup success stories. … These events do a grave disservice to entrepreneurs, startup employees, and investors alike: They congratulate and elevate largely unproven enterprises, they mask the daily struggles of building a startup, and they serve to obfuscate the absolutely vital conversations about a company's integrity and operations."[92]

It's important for every Good Entrepreneur to know that this road isn't all victory cheers and champagne toasts. Businesses go through phases, some easier than others! In my experience, there have been three key phrases of the journey, each marked by its own specific goal: survive, optimize, or thrive.

For most of us, it's difficult just to get past survive!

As discussed in chapter eight, if you are not making a profit, you are firmly in the survival mode. Running a business in survival mode is something that all businesses go through, but Good Entrepreneurs know they can't stay there. You need to use all your resources to get out of this phase. When you are in trouble, you should stop everything and get out of trouble. Even if you can stay open, working on thin margins is often worse than just shutting down and moving on.

This is tricky because the first season of any business is lived in survival mode. You don't know what you don't know, and it will cost your resources to uncover those answers. In some respects, this is exactly what venture capital money is used for: to find previously unknown answers. All investment at this point is trading resources—your time and money—for any answer to the unknown. Because of the sheer number of unknowns you face at the beginning of the journey, survival is always on your mind.

Even if you're not starting a business, you can find yourself in survival mode. Factors outside of our control can swoop in at any moment and knock us over. As the name *survival* suggests, you just have to get through it. You have no choice but to keep on walking. And this is when the entrepreneurial spirit is uncovered—one of determination, quick-thinking, ingenuity, flexibility, and resourcefulness.

In any business, every time the business grows by three times, major components break. The phone system that worked at one hundred thousand dollars in revenue will start to be inefficient at three hundred thousand dollars in revenue. The technology that you built to serve a thousand customers starts to buckle under the weight of three thousand. The shared office space that worked for the first 30 employees will not work for 90. Most entrepreneurs will look at these changes and gladly find a new and better solution. Our ability to leverage these challenges is one of our superpowers.

Good Entrepreneurs let survival mode motivate them to get scrappy and never quit.

DON'T QUIT

There comes a time in the life cycle of every business at which the leader needs to find a way to face the pain. The gauntlet of sleepless nights, the endless migraines, and the seemingly unsolvable problems pile up until they become unmanageable—until they hurt. That's when they must be dealt with in order for Good Entrepreneurs to not only survive but thrive.

As Ben Horowitz puts it, "Whenever I meet a successful CEO, I ask them how they did it. Mediocre CEOs point to their brilliant strategic moves or their intuitive business sense or a variety of other self-congratulatory explanations. The great CEOs tend to be remarkably consistent in their answers. They all say, 'I didn't quit.'"[93]

If we want to be Good Entrepreneurs, then we have to learn not to quit when it gets painful. When you move from the peak to the valley, you have one option to survive, and that is simply not to quit. This is the season that will define you as a leader. It will define the culture—the very DNA of your organization. At this point, you have to make a choice to face the pain, to get scrappy in order to survive, and to stay scrappy in order not to quit.

The problem with being an entrepreneur is that you learn from doing. There is no training module or any other job that can really prepare you to be the person everyone else is looking at you to be. The person who is trying to make purpose out of pain. The person who, sometimes, is just trying to survive. It isn't easy. The reality is choosing not to quit comes with a cost.

I faced this very reality the year I was trying to launch RISE. The pain that came with my fear of failure was real. And in those months of waiting for an answer from Sarah, I was on the verge of quitting several times. But fortunately, I had the support of people like my wife, Angela, who helped me look the pain in the face. And because of that, I didn't quit. I stayed scrappy, and I stayed in the fight. And you know what? Eventually, it paid off.

I'll never forget where I was when I got that phone call. Angela had taken our family out of town to physically remove me from the chaos and mentally recalibrate in this season of survival. We'd escaped to a place where we didn't even have any cell service. I went into town one day to pick up some groceries and saw I had a number of voice mail messages. The only one I cared about was the one with the 202-area code—the one from Washington, DC.

"Hello, Nick. This is Sarah calling, and I have some very good news for you. Your application has been approved, and you are able to start flying."

I fell to my knees and started crying tears of joy in the aisle of the grocery store. I could hardly believe it was real. Of course, I played the message again on speakerphone so Angela could hear and confirm that I wasn't dreaming. We'd survived because we hadn't quit.

DON'T FORCE IT

Now that I'm older, I'm haunted by the number of times I've tried to force my way in life. I've tried to make things happen on my time—when I wanted them to happen and how I wanted them to happen. And truth be told, sometimes it worked, but it didn't last long.

Maybe you've been there. In a season where you'll do anything to survive—to make it to the place you desperately want to get to—it's tempting to take matters into your own hands, isn't it? It's tempting to force it. But the reality is we can only do so much. We can work hard, we can use our resources, we can put our whole hearts into what it is we're after. That's what Good Entrepreneurs do!

But Good Entrepreneurs also know that sometimes the best thing we can do is release our white-knuckle grip from around our goal and trust in what's going to happen next.

My brother-in-law builds beautiful homes in the mountains of Colorado and catches beautiful trout in his spare time. A few years ago, we were floating the Blue River in his boat. I asked him what he likes about floating down the river.

He looked off into the distance and responded, "When I'm on my boat, I'm on river time."

"What is river time?" I asked.

"River time is the speed at which the river flows."

He pointed up ahead where there was a bend in the river about a quarter mile away.

"You see that bend in the river up there? I have no idea what's around that corner, but I'm curious to know. There's almost nothing I can do to get us there faster. The river's flowing at a certain pace, and there's also almost nothing I can do, short of getting out of the river, to get us there slower. So, we're going to get there one way or the other, and the river is going to dictate when we do. And I believe I have the skill to navigate it accordingly. And if not, we'll figure it out."

I've thought about that concept a lot. For most of my life, I've been exhausting myself just trying to change the speed of the river of life. I've been paddling upriver, downriver, and even trying to change the flow of the entire river by creating my own metaphorical dams. So many leaders whom I know do this out of instinct. We believe it's necessary for of our survival.

But if we survive this way, it's usually at the sake of our own wellbeing.

In reality, our efforts to force it rarely make the kind of progress we want. That's why it's important to know how to follow the river. Sometimes, one of the best survival tools a Good Entrepreneur has is to lean into the current and adjust as it moves.

USE YOUR VOICE

If revenue makes you rich, recurring revenue makes you wealthy. That's why our business model at RISE was predicated on recurring revenue.

Our members were charged a monthly fee regardless of how many times they flew. People referred to RISE as the "Uber of airplanes,"[94] and although I appreciated the comparison, I much preferred the "Netflix of airplanes" because Uber is a series of one-off transactions, whereas Netflix fosters a long-term and consistent relationship with its users.

Up until that point at RISE, we had been signing up new members, collecting an initiation fee, and keeping them apprised of our pending launch. Our earliest members who signed up had been waiting the better part of eight months to hear we were cleared to fly. Because of that, many of them thought we weren't ever going to take off and quite a few had even forgotten they'd signed up. So, when we sent out emails to let them know that we were about to start flying and, consequently, begin charging their credit cards, a lot of members asked to opt out. It seemed that in the eight months of waiting, their circumstances had changed.

On top of that, when we started charging the remaining members' credit cards, we started drawing red flags with all the credit card companies because of the large dollar size of the transactions. There are two things credit card company actuaries hate more than anything else: startup companies and airlines.

As you know, we checked both of those boxes.

We started calling our members and asking them to call their credit card companies in order to let the charges through. Admittedly, it wasn't the best look when they had already been waiting months for our promised services. When they did call the credit card companies, they were met with a brief on all the reasons we were risky, but in spite of this warning, the remaining members authorized the charges. They were calls I didn't expect to make, but they helped us survive. I am forever indebted to those members who took a risk on us.

This wasn't the image I had in my mind when I dreamed of finally being able to launch RISE.

We had been set to launch with annual revenue approaching eight figures and ahead of the initial projections, but instead, we found ourselves scrambling to find exactly how much revenue we could count on. Our cash reserves had been depleted waiting for our application to be approved, and since planes are expensive to fly, we had to be precise with the schedule that we flew. But despite the timeline not being what I expected or wanted, I learned that when you use your voice and ask people to help, most of them do.

NOBODY CARES

Do you always get what you want when you ask for it? No. But what happens instead is even better: you build the thick, scrappy skin every Good Entrepreneur needs to survive.

You see, every single one of us started this entrepreneurial journey with a specific vision of what our success would look like. Our culture will be second to none. Our employees will be eager to come to work. We will build a game-changing product that moves the needle and puts a dent in the universe. The final outcome? Well, it's going to be entrepreneurial utopia, of course.

But then, rubber meets the road, and we find out that our vision doesn't match up with reality. At this point, our idea looks nothing like something Steve Jobs or Elon Musk would ever associate with. The product has issues with quality control and customer satisfaction. Customers communicate their frustration. Their confidence in the product, and in us, begins to waver, and the internal gossip begins.

A few employees quit, opting to search for greener grass. Cash is getting dangerously low, and our personal lives are strained. Then, we lose a marquee customer or a competitive bid. Suddenly, survival doesn't seem in sight. Our employees wonder if we have what it takes to be the leader we claimed to be. We wonder the same thing. We're in over our heads. There is no rescue boat coming to save us. No pivot seems possible. No scrappy attitude strong enough to help us survive the voices in our heads.

What happened? Where did the trail zig, and why did we zag? Do we have what it takes to see this through? Are we good enough?

Congratulations! If you have ever found yourself facing this exact feeling, then you aren't alone. In fact, believe it or not, you're likely on the right track. Every Good Entrepreneur has walked this well-worn path before you, and you know what? They've come out on the other side. They've survived.

What's their secret? Well, although there isn't a one-size-fits-all approach, there is one thing I think most successful leaders do that helps them survive moments like this. It's the thing that helps us see clearly amid the fog of the journey so we can make the best move when it seems there are only bad moves. It's the thing that helps us keep going.

The late Raiders owner Al Davis articulated this best in a conversation with his friend and coach of the New York Giants, Bill Parcells. Al had called to check in after the Giants had suffered a slew of injuries.

Parcells relayed his injury issues to Al: "I am just not sure how we can win without so many of our best players. What should I do?"

Davis responded, "Bill, nobody cares, just coach your team."[95]

That might be some of the best survival advice any Good Entrepreneur can get. No one cares about your problems or the excuses you might have. Just find a way to do your job.

Your reasons for giving up and giving in won't preserve one dollar for your investors. They won't save one employee's job or get you one new customer. They especially won't make you feel one bit better when you shut down your company and declare bankruptcy.

All the mental energy you use to elaborate your misery would be far better used trying to find the one seemingly impossible way out of your current mess. Spend zero time on what you *should* have done and devote all your resources to what you are *going to do*. Because in the end, nobody cares how you survive; they just care that you survived.

JUST SURVIVE

When I was younger and quite a few pounds lighter, I participated in an Ironman Triathlon in Florida. In the end, I found the 15 hours that I took to finish the race to be analogous to the journey of the entrepreneur.

It was dusk. I was tired. Exhausted. Ready to stop moving.

I saw a light far away. I kept moving, and the light came closer. I got close enough that I could hear the cheering resonating from the area.

"John, you are an Ironman!"
Cheering. Clapping. Roaring.
"Lisa, you are an Ironman."
Cheering. Clapping. Roaring.

This was the finish line. And I was almost there. Within 150 yards, I would finally be a finisher. All the brutal weekend training sessions—the 20-mile training runs on Saturdays and one-hundred-mile training rides on Sundays. The myriad drinks with the appropriate protein-to-carbohydrate ratio (really more of a mush than a drink). The absolutely soul-crushing experience of training for an Ironman was about to be all worth it.

Since the sun had come up on that Sunday morning at Panama City Beach, I had already swum 2.4 miles in the ocean (and some without goggles, as I'd lost them by getting kicked in the head by another competitor), had ridden 112 miles (most of it with a nasty headwind), and had run, it seemed, the marathon-level 26.2 miles.

I had visions of euphoria in my head.

Until I remembered that I had only concluded one lap of the two-lap marathon. I wasn't nearly as close to the finish line as I thought.

I was so tired, so sore, so done. Yet, I had 13.1 more miles to go. Back out into the dark, by myself.

It was one of the loneliest moments of my life. In that moment, the fear washed over me. Every cell in my body screamed at me to stop. I just wanted it to be over.

It's an uncomfortable feeling, starting deep in your gut. The emotions it brings are visceral. It takes you to places you have never been before—places you never want to go again. And yet, you yearn for it. To see what would happen if we pushed just a little further. To see if we can finish.

Because often it's at this moment—when you're standing on the brink and wondering if you can keep going—that your mind has to take over in order to keep striving for a goal that once seemed implausible, if not impossible.

This is where most people stop. This is where the journey ends. Only the most doggedly persistent continue to the very end—attaining their goal. Jefferson. Jobs. Churchill. Gates. Bonhoeffer. Wilberforce. They heard their callings, and they pursued them, regardless of the pain that occurred along the way, regardless of the fear that told them to quit.

In most employee interviews, I ask this question: What scares you the most in life?

A thoughtful silence typically enters the room. Eyes look off into the distance, and the most remarkable responses flow out of mouths. Often, this is where the spark of truth ignites.

I ask this question because being part of a startup is incredibly scary. There is no room or time for posers. I want to hire someone who has looked into the darkest corners and named their monsters. I want to see depth. I want to see gumption. I want to know that when it gets tough and there's another lap to go, they will go back out into the dark. Even if it's lonely and even if it's scary. One step at a time, they'll stay scrappy until it's finished.

As I neared the end of the second lap of the marathon, I was mentally, emotionally, and physically depleted. But as the lonely, dark night finally gave way to light at the end of the course, I crossed the finish line and heard the words I'd waited for so long to hear.

"Nick, you are an Ironman!"

Instead of feeling elated. I felt like I had just *survived*.

WHEN ENOUGH IS ENOUGH

Here's the thing that makes this difficult as an entrepreneur: You're taught to go until you have nothing left to give. You're taught to continue when mere mortals would stop. You're taught to go on, and go further, and make it more. You're taught exactly what I'm telling you here: to stay scrappy to survive.

But sometimes, you get so far over your ski tips, you can't pull back. You start tumbling down the mountain, but you don't even know that you're tumbling down the mountain. Or maybe you do know that you're tumbling, but you have no choice but to continue to tumble and hope that something will change by some miraculous twist of fate. I saw it happen up close with my own father. He got too far over his ski tips and couldn't stop the eventual fall that was to come.

That's why Good Entrepreneurs must set themselves apart when they're in survival mode. Do you need to face the pain? To not give up? To keep going and keep trying when you're scared? Yes, of course! Every Good Entrepreneur will find themselves at a moment (or more likely, several moments) when they're going to have to decide to get scrappy and do what they have to do. But Good Entrepreneurs know and live their values, vision, and purpose. And that means that if doing what you have to do will cause you to sacrifice any part of these, you'll know it's time to step back and reroute to a better course for not just your business but yourself. That's how you'll ensure that your work—your legacy—will survive intact.

The struggle on this journey is real. But if you can stay scrappy and survive what comes your way, I promise you that you'll be able to look back and be glad you did. You'll stand at the end of that long road and say, "I did it. I made it. I survived."

And you'll be able to say you did it all with the scrappiness of a Good Entrepreneur.

END-OF-CHAPTER HOMEWORK
TEAM COHESION

The goal is to survive, right? Well, one of the things you can do to help you do that is get out of your head and make these lessons real. So, get out your journal, and get your thoughts and emotions out on paper. The brain is powerful, and it can work against you if you are not intentional. Getting the clutter of your head on paper helps you see what's real. Maybe it's not as bad as you imagined it in the echo chamber of your mind. Here in reality, you can name the problem, identify a way out, and begin to execute the plan to help you survive.

Below are six values that will help as you stay scrappy to survive. After reading the value and the definition, give yourself a score from one to 10, with one being the lowest and 10 being perfect.

- *Connected.* Your team needs to feel connected so that you can create a safe environment in which they can feel comfortable to operate. It is up to you to model what this looks like by leading with and showing your own vulnerability. Score 1–10 _____
- *Freedom.* Your team needs the freedom to use their skills to help with attaining the vision. You can support this by being enthusiastic about their good ideas and giving constructive feedback for their less-than-ideal ideas. Score 1–10 _____

- *Pride.* Your team will take responsibility for their projects and the overall success of the organization when they take ownership. Giving them precise guidelines on their roles and responsibilities removes ambiguity and encourages them to be proud of their roles. Score 1–10 _____

- *Tell the truth, or at least don't lie.* In the zone of scrappiness, every bit of energy needs to be used for getting out of survival mode and into optimization. Telling the truth removes unnecessary delays and negative consequences. This seems simple, but it is one of the hardest and most important factors of your success. Facing and resolving negative realities fosters growth and removes false obstacles. Score 1–10 _____

- *Training.* Your team needs consistent training in order to foster growth during this season. Often you don't have the resources to do formal training. That gives you the opportunity to provide hands-on training. What you do in the executive meetings echoes throughout your business. Score 1–10 _____

- *Aligned.* Always question your decisions and actions through the lens of your values, vision, and purpose. If it doesn't serve them, then it needs to be sacrificed for the greater good. Score 1–10 _____

Now, pick the lowest score, and think of a tangible way that you can increase this score over the next quarter. Write down the way you are going to change, and create a plan of action regarding this change.

PRINCIPLE TEN

OPTIMIZE IN ANY SITUATION

FINDING YOUR GROOVE

In emerging from any valley in business (or even in life!), you know you have what it takes to survive. Just like that, you're moving further from chaos and closer to order, finding a balance between the two that will give you a strong foundation on which to build the next phase of this thing. You're firmly headed in the right direction now. You've officially found your groove.

Now, the question for every Good Entrepreneur is this: How do you keep this up? In other words, how do you stay in this groove? Because once you've found it, you don't want to lose it!

I think the secret for anyone in this season of business or life is to pause and reflect. Look at what has worked, consider what hasn't worked, think about the things you have in front of you to build on, and decide how you want to grow.

As you do, it's imperative that you put systems in place to track your progress. I am a fan of using electronic dashboards to track, in real time, the key metrics of my businesses. The main dashboard should correspond to what your long-term goals are and, at a minimum, should give you insight into your sales, inventory, profit margin, customer satisfaction, and employee satisfaction. Tracking these metrics will give you a chance to see what's working well and what isn't in these specific areas. Beyond these items, you can get more precise. For example, we had a specific goal for passenger load on our planes. At our goal level, we would be maximizing profit, so we tracked every flight load in order to see how we were doing against our goals.

The dashboard and goals can evolve over time, but when you are in this season of building your business, it is critical to track how you are doing as you go. This may seem obvious or even elementary to some, but it's critical to understanding where you are and where you want to be as Good Entrepreneurs. You have to understand the groove you're in if you want to not only stay in it but grow from it. Having a firm grasp on the core metrics of your business will help you do just that.

Then, share these metrics within your business. You are not a lone ranger, and you cannot do all of the things necessary to be successful on your own. You have to rely on your employees to do their jobs. You have to trust the people you've put around you to support you. By providing them feedback in the form of black-and-white numbers, you are helping them see how their work affects the rest of the organization. You're giving them goals to work toward and helping them find their own personal groove in their work.

It's important to note that although knowing and tracking what's happening in your business is key for growth and development, it isn't always an indicator of what's to come. So many things can crop up that are simply out of your control or that you couldn't have seen coming. And then, through no fault of your own, a crack is introduced into the foundation you've created.

Maybe you know this from experience. I certainly do! As I'm writing this book, I do so in quarantine because of the COVID-19 global pandemic. Many of my friends are on the brink of losing it all. One day, they were successfully moving ahead—working in their groove—and the very next, they were forced to shut down, stop production, or close up shop. Now, they're scrambling to find a way to survive. Could they have prevented this? Controlled it? Seen it coming? None of us could! Like so many of us in this season, they're standing in the midst of circumstances beyond their control, forced to find a new groove in a world of uncertainty.

KEEP IT SIMPLE

Here's the good news I want every Good Entrepreneur to know. Whether you're facing circumstances or challenges within your control or not, there's always something you can do to optimize.

How do you go about optimizing when there are so many places to start?

Steve Jobs gave us an answer: "Simple can be harder than complex; you have to work hard to get your thinking clean to make it simple. But it's worth it in the end because once you get there, you can move mountains."[96]

In other words, think simple. Start there—with the simplest piece of the puzzle—and optimize.

Now, I know this isn't as easy as it sounds. There is a tendency in business to try to make something that should be simple into something that is very complex. Good Entrepreneurs need to avoid this pitfall. We need to change our thinking so that we work smarter, not harder. We need to focus on keeping it simple.

My friend Trey says, "Business isn't easy, but it is simple." All business is, at its most basic level, is one human offering a product or service to another human. The product itself can be incredibly complex, but the role of business need not be. When you find yourself getting wrapped up in seemingly complex issues, it's time to take a pause and reflect on what led you there. What can you do to get back to *simple*?

This is where the values, vision, and purpose you've laid out for yourself as a Good Entrepreneur in chapter seven can be helpful. They are the road maps back to simple. When things feel out of control, or overwhelming, or you're lost in the weeds of complexity, think about your values, vision, and purpose. Are the things that have caused you stress or overcomplicated your business aligned with your values, vision, and purpose? Chances are, at least in some way, you've gotten off course. Looking at your situation or circumstance through the lens of your values, vision, and purpose will help you see what in your life or business isn't lining up with what you want for yourself. It will help you know where you need to get back on track.

Pilots use a host of instruments that give real-time feedback, allowing for adjustments to be made based on the information they receive. But before Jimmy Doolittle became the first pilot to take off, fly, and land using these instruments alone in 1929,[97] pilots were left to fly using their own five senses. As you can imagine, this severely limited the information they could rely on to make life and death decisions. Your values, vision, and purpose are those instruments for you. And to ignore them when things get complicated would be the equivalent of flying at night in the middle of a thunderstorm and hoping you land safely.

In other words, it wouldn't be wise!

LEAN INTO CHANGE

One of the best ways to optimize in your business is to lean into change. The work of a Good Entrepreneur should always be growing and developing. And while the standards you have for your work—the values, vision, and purpose—can remain the same, the way you go about achieving your goals shouldn't be static. In fact, Good Entrepreneurs should lean into change as a way to grow and get better on their journey.

At RISE, we had an amazing team working hard to maintain our vision, values, and purpose. Of course, we had some missteps. In fact, we made many poor decisions simply because we didn't always know what we were doing, but that's just the way I wanted it. I knew how quickly organizations could start to atrophy when the most common refrain was "Well, that's the way we've always done it." I wanted us to be open to new ideas, new ways of doing things, and new goals. I wanted to be open to change.

I created a rule at RISE that I didn't want to hire anyone from the airline industry (with pilots and maintenance professionals being the exception). We were trying to set ourselves apart from the commercial airline industry, and because of that, I didn't want their influence on our culture. I didn't want to hear "Well, that's the way we've always done it" from anyone. Because as far as I was concerned, we were going to do something new and far better than what the commercial airlines were doing.

Living in Dallas, home to both Southwest and American Airlines, we had plenty of people with a background in the industry apply to work at RISE. And for the most part, I held to my conviction. But at one point, I had to be willing to lean into change if I wanted to hire someone who could help us optimize.

One of my employees first heard of RISE while working at a large airline. When she heard about the rule we had to avoid bringing on anyone from that industry, she promptly quit her job and called to let me know she did just that. To be honest, I was impressed. And because of her sheer tenacity, I hired her. She had a spark in her that she wasn't afraid to unleash when needed and a courage to take a risk that makes for a bold employee. If I wasn't willing to lean into change and make an exception to my own rule, we would've missed out on having her as a part of our team.

Not all change is good for you or your business. But being able to identify the kind of change that will help you optimize is important for Good Entrepreneurs. Because when we can lean into that kind of change, we're leaning into what makes both ourselves and our businesses better.

PEOPLE AND PROFIT

The customer is always right is a common phrase in business. Entrepreneurs focus on customer satisfaction to ensure the happiness of their customers. I used to repeat this phrase often in my career, bending over backward to make sure the customer was always happy. Why? Because they were the ones providing for the business by increasing our revenue.

But as any Good Entrepreneur knows, this mantra can only take you so far—because the customer can't be right at the expense of the values, vision, and purpose you have for your business. Your customer can't be right at the cost of your integrity. Customer satisfaction is a key to optimization, but it can't be held at such a high regard that it costs you that optimization. You can't hold your profit over your people.

In *Nuts!: Southwest Airlines' Crazy Recipe for Business and Personal Success*, authors Kevin and Jackie Freiberg tell the story of the growth of Southwest airlines and their unconventional and fearless leader, Herb Kelleher.[98] In one particular story, they speak of a woman who frequently flew on Southwest but was disappointed with every aspect of the company's operation. In fact, she became known as the "Pen Pal" because after every flight, she wrote in with a complaint. She didn't like the fact that the company didn't assign seats. She didn't like the absence of a first-class section. She didn't like not having a meal in flight. She didn't like Southwest's boarding procedure. She didn't like the flight attendants' sporty uniforms and the casual atmosphere. And she hated peanuts! But it was her last letter, reciting a litany of complaints, that momentarily stumped Southwest's customer relations people. The book explains: "Southwest prides itself on answering every letter that comes to the company and several employees tried to respond to this customer, patiently explaining why we do things the way we do them. [Our response] was quickly becoming a [large] volume until they bumped it up to Herb's desk, with a note: 'This one's yours.' In sixty seconds, Kelleher wrote back and said, 'Dear Mrs. Crabapple, we will miss you. Love, Herb.'"[99]

I had the opportunity to meet Herb on several occasions, and he was consistently the instigator that I wanted him to be. Even though I didn't know him well, I thought of him as a mentor and read everything I could about him while constantly quizzing my friends who worked with him. And eventually, that study paid off on a random Thursday afternoon when I got the chance to channel my inner Herb.

"Nick, we need to talk."

This was how I was greeted by our director of customer success when he walked into my office that day.

"One of our members just screamed at one of our employees, and now our employee is crying in the bathroom. I don't have the full story yet, but I thought you would want to know."

We had just started flying, so we didn't know what we didn't know. We were dealing with the consequences of bad decisions left and right, working tirelessly to correct them and dial in the customer service aspect of running an airline. Every day I came into work, I was filled with embarrassment about all the disparaging things I used to say about the legacy airlines I flew almost every week. As it turned out, running an airline isn't easy, and it certainly isn't for the faint of heart.

Of course, customer satisfaction was a big deal to us in those days! It had to be if we wanted to keep going and growing. But as I sat in my office that day thinking about my employee crying in the bathroom, I remembered our purpose statement: "RISE exists to take care of its employees." If I truly wanted to optimize this business, I had to stay true to that purpose, both in theory and in practice.

I called the crying employee and asked her to come to my office. When she entered, she had stopped crying, but the red around her eyes and disheveled eyeliner betrayed her best attempt to collect herself. I knew this woman well, so I knew she was not easily thrown off or frustrated. If she was in this state, something bad must have happened.

"What happened?" I asked.

"It's really not that big of a deal. One of our members was upset at a delayed plane, and I think he was just having a bad day," she said quietly.

"Who was the member?" I asked.

She responded with the name and now it was my turn to take a deep breath. The member in question was not our most famous member, but he held his own in most areas of his life, as his overwhelming wealth testified. But was his clout worth sacrificing the wellbeing of our people? Our values, vision, and purpose?

A Good Entrepreneur would say it wasn't.

Looking directly into my employee's eyes, I said, "I need to know exactly what he said to you."

Her eyes widened, and her face went flush. "Everything?"

"Everything," I confirmed.

She stiffened her back and recounted the conversation word for word. His words were vulgar, pathetic, and mostly childish. In short, he was an adult throwing a temper tantrum because he didn't get what he wanted. Years of indulgence had taught this man that he could raise his voice and throw his weight and wallet around to get what he wanted. I didn't want that to be true at RISE.

I thanked the employee, asked her to take the rest of the day off to recover, and prepared for the next conversation I needed to have. I closed the door to my office and dialed the number of this high-powered executive, trying not to think of the revenue we were about to lose as I broke up with this valuable customer. I let out a sigh of relief when I got his voice mail. At least he wouldn't be able to argue with me.

"Hi, this is Nick Kennedy, the CEO of RISE. I understand that you were upset with a recent interaction with our company, and I'm terribly sorry for the inconvenience that our issue caused you. With that said, I just had a conversation with my employee whom you spoke to, and she told me, in detail, what you said to her. Now I don't pretend to know what would cause you to be so mean to anyone—much less a woman your daughter's age who was trying to help you. That type of behavior is not allowed at RISE. We appreciate your business with us, but I am canceling your membership effective today and refunding your money. I wish you the best of luck in the future."

I hung up the phone, took a deep breath, called my controller, and asked her to refund the money that we so desperately needed. Was losing that money going to help us optimize the business? Not on paper. But in the long run, it would because it meant that we didn't sacrifice our people or their value along the way.

A few long minutes later, my phone rang. It was the member returning my call.

"This is Nick," I answered.

Before I could get another word out, the boisterous voice of this now-former member cut in.

"Nick, I loved your service so much. I didn't know how I could love it anymore, but the fact that you stood up to me being a bully on behalf of your employee makes me love it even more. It's been years since someone called me out like that, but man, you are so right. I am in the wrong. Can I please stay on as a member? I am so sorry."

I was dumbfounded. If you had given me a hundred options of how this guy would've responded, this would have been number 99 on the list. I quickly thought back to our values. The first one was love. I truly believe you can't love someone until you know them, so I wanted to create the opportunity for this member to do just that. To see my employee as a person, not just someone who served him. To know that employee so he could treat them with value going forward.

"You didn't offend me," I responded, "you offended my employee. She is the one who needs the apology here."

"If I do that, can I continue to fly?" he pleaded.

"That's really up to her. Let me speak to her and see if she is willing to talk to you after the way you spoke to her today."

With that, we ended our call.

I quickly called our employee and explained the situation.

"You're leaving it up to me to decide if he can come back?" she asked, confused.

"Yes," I told her confidently. "The offense was toward you, not me. Therefore, you have total control over the situation. You don't have to speak with him, but I think it would be good for you to do so."

Within a few short hours, the power dynamic had flipped. Now, this fresh-out-of-college woman held the power over the seasoned executive.

"Sure, it's okay for him to call me," she replied.

And he did. He apologized profusely, and she gave him grace, allowing him to become a member once again. In fact, he went on to become one of our best members.

I wish I had the insight to think about these types of situations when we developed our values, vision, and purpose, but the truth is I didn't know what was ahead. But what I did know was what it felt like to be on the receiving end of so many abusive employers. I knew how it felt to deal with unethical, unkind, and immature bosses. And I knew that in the end, that wasn't the way to optimize your business or your people. So, I made a commitment to the people I had the privilege of leading to be a different kind of leader. I had a set of principles that I could filter these types of situations through to determine the best response—the response that valued people over profit.

And this principle doesn't just extend to others. It applies to you, the leader, as well.

Ray Dalio is a legendary investor and leader of Bridgewater Associates based in Connecticut. Talk to anybody in the investment community, and they will tell you that Bridgewater has one of the strongest cultures in their industry. In his book *Principles*, he outlines a set of over two hundred principles that influence how he runs his life and business.[100] Although Bridgewater manages money, the principles don't contain a word about investing. They are rules for how to act and think in any situation you might face. They focus on building meaningful work and relationships. They range from the philosophical ("Realize you have nothing to fear from truth.") to the practical ("Recognize that behavior modification typically takes about 18 months of constant reinforcement.").

Although he has been called the guru of investing, he encourages employees to communicate with him as a peer. Here's an email that a client adviser sent to him after a meeting with an important potential client:

"Ray—you deserve a 'D–' for your performance today. ... You rambled for 50 minutes. ... It was obvious to all of us that you did not prepare at all, because there is no way you could have been that disorganized at the outset if you had prepared."

Truthfully, what would you do if one of your employees sent that email to you? I know that in my weaker moments, I would have come unglued and begun the firing process. It takes discipline to stay engaged in that moment and refer back the values that you put in place. But a Good Entrepreneur would do just that. They'd pause and reflect. They'd consider if the facts of this email were accurate. And they'd think about how they can own their poor decisions and take the criticism to change where needed. In other words, they'd value the words of their people.

Choosing people over short-term profit isn't easy. In fact,[101] sometimes it feels impossible. When money is low and the potential profit you stand to gain is high, it would be easy to forsake the people around you. But Good Entrepreneurs know that in order to optimize their business for the long haul, they need to create long-term profit by creating a business that will last. They need values, vision, and purpose. And they need the people around them to hold them to that.

READING YOUR OWN PRESS

Optimizing with our values, vision, and purpose in mind doesn't just help us keep others in check; it keeps us, the Good Entrepreneurs, in check as well.

During my time with RISE, we had lots of articles written about us. About a dozen were selected to be hung in the lobby of our office, and out of that dozen, I kept one that still hangs in my office today. *The New York Times* wrote an article about our burgeoning industry and published with it a picture of me laughing with my customer and friend Ben Lamm in front of one of our planes,[102] and it made the front page of the business section. The article was an honest look at where we were at the time. It detailed what our struggles were and what we needed to do in order to continue our success.

In all the other interviews I did, I would tell the reporter a story, and they would write a story that reflected exactly what I had told them. I was quickly starting to understand why they called these pieces of journalism "puff pieces." They were there to puff up the ego of the leaders, and that's exactly what they did. Rarely was I challenged in my bravado in these interviews, and when I was, I was quickly able to convince the reporter of my side of the story. I was glad to have it this way, but I was also sad to know that this was the state of journalism. These reporters who had dreamed of one day winning a Pulitzer for investigative journalism were now writing puff pieces for a paycheck.

The New York Times reporter, on the other hand, asked hard questions multiple times and from multiple angles. They were in a class all by themselves. They wanted sources, they wanted references, and they wanted it all documented precisely for their scrutiny. But the article that came out as a result of all that is the one I want hanging in my office. Because if I'm going to read my own press, I want it to be realistic. A puff piece isn't going to help me stay the course of the Good Entrepreneur, but a realistic and even scrutinizing look at both myself and my company certainly is.

Here's the problem with reading your own press: eventually, you start to believe it. In the midst of the chaos of growing your business, you're inevitably going to face challenges and make poor decisions. Those moments can cause you to question everything. They can lead you to look for validation anywhere you can find it. Sure, the best thing would be to ask mensches, employees, mentors, or even family for the reality check you need. But the far easier (and more tempting) thing to do is walk out of your office, stand in front of the wall of press, and gaze into the carefully crafted image you've created for yourself. To read a few of the headlines and be reminded about what a genius you are. To buy into the puff piece version of yourself to validate who you are and what you've done. There is less pain in believing your own press than there is in having the hard conversations necessary to see the truth of the situation. But Good Entrepreneurs know they must choose the latter of the two if they want to optimize themselves as leaders.

I now work as an advisor for leaders, entrepreneurs, and businesses. When I am called into an organization, I spend time with both the leaders and employees to simply listen. I listen for a pattern to emerge that tells me the real story of the organization. I listen past the puff piece they may be trying to write. I'm always most impressed with the leaders who bring me in and speak openly from the start. Why? Because they have the courage to move beyond their egos to hear what's really going on in their business. They have the desire to do this work right, and because of that, they're always the first and fastest to help optimize.

REMEMBER YOUR WHY

The values, vision, and purpose that help you optimize and grow your work as a Good Entrepreneur? They're born out of your why. And because of that, they'll help you remember your why as you go forward in optimizing your work for success.

When I started RISE, I had a huge hole in my heart because of the absence of my father. The why behind RISE was born out of that place. It wasn't about giving people access to private planes; it was about giving them back their seats at the dinner table with their families. We were providing a way to avoid the laborious airport process and give them back all the time that process stole from them each year. We were making it possible for families to spend more time together and for relationships to flourish. We were replacing the absence I felt as a kid with the ability and time to be present.

That was our vision—our why—and we did it. We did it really well—so well that we were written up in *The New York Times*, *The Wall Street Journal*, *USA Today*, and many other publications. I even won the Ernst and Young Entrepreneur of The Year award.[103] Those were, of course, great honors to receive, but they weren't the greatest accomplishments of my time at RISE. They weren't why we kept going, growing, and optimizing.

> The time I got back with my own family.
> The time our members gave to their own relationships.
> The people whose lives were made better because of what we did.
> Those were the whys that kept us going.

Some people have asked me if I feel different about entrepreneurship now that I've gone through this process, and the truth is, I do. Preparation, scrappiness, and determination were the three main characteristics that helped me achieve the success I have seen. Those are still skills I think are necessary to help any Good Entrepreneur look out into the universe and believe that they can do something that no one else has ever done before.

They are the things you need to help you get started, survive, optimize, and eventually thrive in this race.

But now I'd say that none of those things matter without values, vision, and purpose. I was so wounded by the absence of my father that I was willing to risk almost everything I had so that other kids wouldn't have that same experience. That purpose is what motivated us. It's what defined our vision and our values. And that's what ultimately gave us success.

Anyone can optimize their business. But Good Entrepreneurs know that real success isn't just about profit. Real success is about aligning your values, vision, and purpose to meet a need that will make an impact not just in your life but in the lives of many others.

That's how you optimize. That's how you thrive.

END-OF-CHAPTER HOMEWORK
WHAT IS YOUR WHY?

Take out your journal and write down your why. In order to help get to your why, answer the following questions:

- What is the reason you want to be an entrepreneur?
- Why are you willing to go through the painful process of building a business?'
- What is the mission of your business (reference chapter seven)?
- What will you need to remember, when the journey turns dark and tumultuous, to remind you to keep going?
- Who are you willing to share these answers with to receive feedback?

PRINCIPLE ELEVEN

THRIVE IN BUSINESS AND IN LIFE

GETTING EVERYTHING YOU WANT

On the morning *The Wall Street Journal* published an article on what we had built at RISE,[104] I was empty inside. Not too long before, Scott McCartney, the famed aviation reporter for the *WSJ*, had sat in my office overlooking runway 31L at Love Field in Dallas to discuss our business and the overall future of aviation. Although hesitant to give us more kudos than we deserved, he was aligned with us in regard to what was broken in the industry and was interested in how RISE was trying to fix it. It was the ultimate validation to receive from someone in the aviation world. While he validated our vision, he also validated my belief that anyone could enter an industry and create positive change, regardless of where they came from.

If you had told me that in a few short years this idea born out of an office above my garage and refined by an incredible team would get us to this point, I would've told you that you were crazy. I wanted it badly, but I also knew actually getting it was a long shot.

But then it happened. It actually happened. It was almost everything I had wanted.

Any Good Entrepreneur who's felt that feeling knows what I mean. We were a way off from our final goal, but we were also well on the road to getting there, having survived the most treacherous time for most businesses. To have crossed the chasm. To see your dream become a reality. Well, there's no feeling like it, is there? Getting everything you want sure does seem like thriving.

The only problem? Sometimes it doesn't mean we're *actually* thriving.

At the height of my success with RISE, I was professionally where I wanted to be; however, personally, my world was crumbling. Although my business continued to optimize, I was on the brink of losing just about everything else.

That's what happens when you put everything—maybe even too much—into your work. You forget that there's a bigger world with other people and important priorities in it that need your attention too. And Good Entrepreneurs know that in order to truly thrive, they can't forsake one for the sake of the other.

AN INVESTMENT

CEOs have a couple of main responsibilities that are uniquely theirs to own. First, they have to understand what's around the corner and be able to communicate that to the team. Then they have to create and uphold the values, vision, and purpose of the organization. Finally, they also make sure you don't run out of cash!

At RISE, I painted a vision for our future and communicated that well, and we had values, vision, and purpose dialed in. In those places, we were thriving. But that last one? Well, the reality is we were undercapitalized from day one. Planes are incredibly expensive to operate, and because of that, we had to find creative ways to stretch our cash and function as a company without ever really having a way to pour fuel on the marketing fire so that we could grow our business.

In short, I became a professional fundraiser in those days, and I hated it. This was not where I thrived. Raising capital was the thing I disliked most about starting RISE. Truth be told, I was pretty good at it. I believed deeply in the service we provided and was able to passionately articulate that to gain the trust of investors to support us. That is the upside of raising money.

The downside is that when you raise money, you owe money. When an investor buys into your company, they rightfully expect to see a return on that investment. And although this is the fair deal I signed up for when pitching RISE to investors, it wasn't one I was mentally prepared to handle. I was unaware of the psychological trauma this expectation would have on me.

When it comes to paying back investors, intent is usually disregarded. In most scenarios, if an investor or customer loses money in an investment, they don't care if you *intended* to defraud them; they just want their money back. And in the event that they can't get that, then they want someone to pay a price for what they lost. Money was a trigger to me. I had witnessed when my father went to prison just how quickly you can go from top to bottom, and because that, I had a tendency to control every aspect of the business as if my freedom depended on it.

Sure, their investments were helping our business launch and grow, but the stress of knowing they had a financial stake and an expectation of return wasn't allowing me to thrive at all personally.

My largest investor, who was a dear friend and wise businessman, could eventually sense my stress. When he asked how I was doing one day, I gave him the standard reply.

"Oh, you know, things could be better, but I'm not complaining either."

I wasn't lying, but I also wasn't giving him the whole truth. And because he knew me, he saw right through it.

"No, Nick, how are you really doing?" He pressed. "I can sense a change in your personality. You aren't having much fun doing this, are you?"

And then, the floodgates opened. I came clean, telling him about my stress level, my fears, my work, and the toll they were taking on me and my family. It was the most honest I'd been with anyone about how little I was thriving at the time.

Once I finished speaking, my friend said, "Nick, I don't want this to sound pretentious at all, but if you lose all of the money that I have invested in RISE, it will not change my lifestyle one bit. I feel weird saying that to you, but I need you to relax a little bit so that you can have a clear mind in order to make prudent, strategic decisions for the company."

I felt like a hundred-pound weight had been lifted off my shoulders. One simple sentence gave me the freedom I needed to loosen my grip and lower my stress. It gave me permission to find a better way. It opened up the door so that I could start to thrive.

Looking back at that time, I am in awe of how big a part my personal issues played into my level of stress and anxiety around RISE. I had seen my father's fall from grace and unknowingly taken it on as a part of my own identity. It created an enormous sense of pressure that made it impossible for me to truly thrive as an entrepreneur. Being given even the smallest permission to take off some of that pressure changed the game for me.

As Good Entrepreneurs, we have to be able to see where we're struggling. We have to be honest with ourselves about what's standing in the way of our ability to thrive. And when we can't, we have to listen to voices like the one of my friend and investor, voices that give us permission to take off the pressure and let it go.

Then we can start to thrive.

LET IT GO

One of the most difficult parts about learning to thrive is that sometimes it requires us to walk away. In order to thrive as Good Entrepreneurs, we have to be willing and ready to let it all go.

We had done an amazing job of getting RISE off the ground, both literally and figuratively. But I knew that I had to find a way to land the plane on behalf of all of my stakeholders. Luckily for us, there was a well-capitalized competitor who wanted to get into the Texas market. We started initial discussions about them acquiring our company. They immediately recognized the value of our business, and very quickly, things progressed.

During this time, I had to face the reality that RISE was not going to be my final act on this Earth. I wouldn't be running an airline that millions of people would fly on. It's what I desired—what I dreamed RISE would become—but it wasn't going to happen that way, at least not with me as its CEO. I had to acknowledge my own limitations. It was time for me to let it go.

Selling the company you've built is a lot of things, but *fun* is not one of the words I would use to describe the process. The other airline presented a term sheet, and negotiations began. We went back and forth a few times, working to get to a position where both parties were happy. And in the end, although neither side got everything they wanted, we both got to the ultimate goal. Just like that, the sale was in motion.

Shortly thereafter, we began the due diligence process. Due diligence is a process where all the relevant information needed to verify the terms of the deal is shared. The goal is to uncover any hidden details that could possibly derail the deal. During this stage, the buyer gets to meet key employees, verify the books, evaluate the assets, review the liabilities, and basically get information on anything else that could be used to value the company. It's an incredibly laborious and invasive process that is nothing short of a paperwork nightmare. Thousands of pages of documents are generated, reviewed, edited, and sent to the other party. It's intense, and everyone is holding their breath the whole time, not wanting to upset the progress made to get the deal done.

Every time I think about getting deals done, I am reminded about a story my friend Gary told me about a deal he was working on several years ago. Gary had strategically moved the deal up the ladder at a large health care system for approval from the chief information officer (CIO). The legal teams had signed off on the deal, but the day before the signing was to take place, the CIO had a major health setback. He was hospitalized and never returned to work. That deal was within 12 hours of being signed and had crossed all the major thresholds, the only exception being the necessary signature. Gary never got the deal signed. And that story always reminds me that, in reality, no deal is done until it's signed.

But eventually, the deal at RISE was signed. It was done. And it was time for me to let it go. Was it easy? Of course not! Any Good Entrepreneur knows how much blood, sweat, and tears goes into building and living out your dream. So, making the decision to let it go wouldn't be easy for any of us. But when you know what's at stake, letting it go gets a little easier.

For me, the health and wellbeing of not just myself but my family was on the line. And if we wanted to find a way to thrive, I had to be willing to walk away.

A WHISPER

The stress at RISE was taxing, but my personal life was downright exhausting. I had climbed an impossibly tall mountain, founding, building, and selling an airline. Very few people on the face of the Earth could claim the same, and yet inside, I didn't feel the joy that I thought I would. In fact, I felt the complete opposite.

I was empty.

For over 10 years, Angela and I have participated in a community group at our church. The purpose of this group is straightforward: we aim to live life together in a community of love and redemption. Every Sunday night, a group of nearly 40 people representing seven families converge on our house. The kids swim or watch a movie while the adults share what is going on in our lives. Afterward, we have dinner and continue the conversation. This group has been instrumental in our lives, through the good times and the bad times. They have been the shoulders we've leaned on more times than I can count. It is no small feat that we have been together for so long, and one of the reasons I think it's worked is because we have chosen to be vulnerable with each other. We lay it all out there, refusing to let shame enter the conversation. We encourage one another to thrive.

We have a tradition of having everyone in the group share their four *H*s: history, heroes, high times, and hard times. Each member of the group stands up and shares a little bit of their life story through this lens. We've actively chosen to love each other unconditionally, giving grace to each other as we walk through our journeys. We've created an environment of vulnerability in our community group that allows us to share the story that lives inside of us and, in doing so, connect with each other on a unique level. The process of the four *H*s helps remove things like secrecy, silence, and judgment and replace them with empathy.

A few years ago, we had a new family join our group. We began the new relationship by introducing ourselves using our trusted process of the four *H*s. I asked one particular member of the group several times if they would like to share their story at the next meeting, but they always came back with an excuse. Finally, when everyone else had shared, this member had no choice but to go next. She opened up about her father and his life filled with bad decisions that brought much embarrassment and shame to her. This man had indeed made many decisions that caused much harm to his family, but my friend had risen above this, created a beautiful path for herself, and became a better version of her father. Now, she was able to thrive. It was a beautiful story, and I was thankful she found the courage to share it.

After the meeting, I approached her to thank her for the generous gift she gave us in sharing her story with vulnerability.

"I have to ask you a question," I said. "Your story is beautiful and moving, but it seemed like you were hesitant to tell it. Was there any particular reason?"

Through tears, she said, "I am so embarrassed that my father is a reflection on me. I was afraid of what everyone else would think."

Without hesitation, I responded, "Oh, friend, your father's actions and consequences are his alone. He is no reflection on you."

As soon as the words left my lips, I heard an audible voice that wasn't mine saying the same words at the same time. My words spoken back to me in a mere whisper.

At that moment, I realized that the truth that was being spoken to my friend was meant for me too.

My father isn't a reflection on me.

That audible whisper into my ear began to penetrate my heart. It slowly pried open the emotional vault that I had locked years ago. It filled up some of the spaces that had felt so empty in me. And it paved the way for me to find the freedom to thrive.

Being a Good Entrepreneur isn't just about thriving in your work; it's about thriving as a person. If you want to stay the course of the Good Entrepreneur, you have to open yourself up to deal with what may be holding you back. You have to listen to the gentle whispers that tell you the truth. And you have to let that truth begin to set you free.

I SEE YOU

I wasn't the only one facing the fallout of my personal struggles. Angela was feeling the weight of it too, and our marriage was paying the price. Angela is a physician who, at the time, was homeschooling our kids while I was working on RISE. The stress of this life began to grow until we were on the verge of a break. We weren't thriving in our relationship; instead, we were simply tolerating each other.

We had taken the kids to Big Bend National Park that year, trying to make some family fun on vacation. But there in the shower of our hotel room, Angela and I had the biggest fight of our lives. We were both naked, but we fought as if we had on the armor of a thousand armies. It was ugly, it was unkind, and we knew it was a sign that something was really wrong. We didn't know where to turn for help, and honestly, I don't know that we even wanted help at that point.

Luckily, we had some mensches who saw the unraveling of our marriage happening. They saw that we were living with little more than tolerance, and they stepped in to encourage us to seek counsel. I was wary of this option, thinking I was more than capable of working through my problems on my own. But as a peace offering to my wife, I agreed to give it a shot.

At our first session we found ourselves in a heated discussion when our counselor looked at Angela and said, "Why don't you tell Nick that you see him?"

Silence hung in the air.

"Wait, you want me to say, 'I see you?' Why would you want that?" Angela asked.

"Just try it."

A bewildered look crossed my wife's face. I'm sure an even more confused look rested on my face. We had been married nearly two decades at that point, but I don't think that we had ever uttered this phrase to each other. It was weak. It was ambiguous. It was milk toast in verbal form. But since we were paying through the nose for this conversation, Angela did exactly as she was asked.

"Okay," she said, turning to me. "Um, I see you."

Of all the scenarios we'd encountered together, we rarely found ourselves feeling awkward around one another—that is, until this moment. Again, silence hung in the air. And then, something magical happened.

With a breath of fresh empathy, Angela continued.

"I see who you are, what drives you, what you long for, what scares you, and what you are trying to be. I see your secrets and your silence, and I don't judge you. I have empathy for you. I see you."

It felt like a 2-by-4 hit me across the head. In my 40 years on this Earth, I don't know that I've ever had anyone say something so profound to me.

I see you.

Those three words opened me up. They opened my eyes to what I needed. I needed to be seen, acknowledged, and known for something beyond my accomplishments. I needed those things to thrive.

And there was Angela, ready to give them to me.

I was so broken, and I didn't even know it. I lived in this illusion that my life hadn't fallen apart decades ago when my father went to prison. I lived in this illusion that I could somehow keep everything together on my own. I lived in this illusion that my business success meant I was finally thriving.

But Angela saw through it. She saw what was real. She saw who I was. She saw what I needed. And she helped me see it too.

After years of carefully constructing the perfect life filled with almost everything a man could want, I realized in that moment that my net worth had absolutely nothing to do with my true worth.

If you want to thrive as a Good Entrepreneur, you have to find your true worth. You have to see yourself and your life as the culmination of things that matter. You have to find others who will see those things in you when you can't see them yourself.

Our real ability to thrive isn't about our net worth; it's about our true worth.

RICHARD HOFFMAN

My friend Tom is one of the most intentional people I know. He listens intently and then really thinks before providing feedback on the topic at hand. Over the course of several years, Tom had recommended that I participate in a program at our church that would allow me to get real with myself. My pride told me I didn't need the help, but in reality, I was exhausted and approaching rock bottom during this season. At the insistence of Angela, I joined the program.

The leader of our group was a man named Richard Hoffman. Richard was a man who had seen some stuff in his life. He was very open with his faults, and although they aren't mine to share, you can believe me when I tell you that he did not resemble the typical evangelical Christian from Dallas. At that time, he was rough, broken, and well aware of his weaknesses. But he shared them liberally with us. He always told the truth. He didn't care who was listening; if truth needed to be spoken, it would be spoken. Richard often told me that I reminded him of a younger version of himself—sometimes wrong but never in doubt. I don't think he meant it as a compliment.

That was Richard *before* he was diagnosed with stage four pancreatic cancer—a virtual death sentence cast down from the cells within his body. Richard was diagnosed shortly after we met, and if he didn't care what you thought of him before his diagnosis, he certainly didn't care after his chemotherapy started.

Every Wednesday night, Richard, a handful of other men, and I showed up to meet. Those first few weeks, I was diligent but lost. The lessons were pertinent and good, but I remember writing down answers in my workbook that seemed to be out of sync with the rest of the group.

For a large part of my life, I have over-indexed in reading personalities so that I could transform into a chameleon. I knew how to show other people who I wanted to be or who I thought they would be impressed with. One step ahead meant that I could escape from my weaknesses in their presence. I had perfected this act, and because of that, it was rare that I couldn't come up with a good answer. But this experience had me discombobulated. As we went around the room sharing our answers, I found myself out of sync with the rest of the men, frantically changing my answers in real time based on the evolving questions.

Several weeks in, I was sitting on my back porch writing in my workbook when I came across a question that went something like this: How likely are you to ask God for help?

I thought about the question for approximately seven seconds and decided on the spot to aim for humor over honesty.

"He's lucky if he's in the top 10 options! I have the 'Nick Kennedy top-10 go-to' moves, and only if they don't work (and they almost always work) do I ask God to help a brother out."

I finished the lesson and didn't think much about it until I showed up that night to meet.

Richard opened our meeting that night the way he always did.

"My name is Richard, and this time I am feeling_____."

The blank was to be filled with one of the eight key emotions: anger, fear, sadness, disgust, surprise, anticipation, joy, and shame. This whole ritual was weird and uncomfortable to me. I convinced myself at the time it was because I thought emotions were for the weak, but really, I was compensating for the fact that not only did I not know that there were eight basic emotions, but I also had no idea what I felt at any given time. I was numb.

After we all filled in the blank for ourselves, we moved to the lesson for that week. The first couple of questions were answered by others in the group, but when it came to me, Richard asked, "How likely are you to ask God for help?"

I paused for dramatic effect, slowly articulated my answer, and sat back, waiting for the room to begin laughing. *Because if I can make you laugh, I can make you love me.* But here, silence reigned in the room. Only the flickering of the fluorescent lights could be heard until Richard finally opened his mouth.

"Are you serious?" he asked with an intensity I had yet to see.

I realized immediately that I had stepped into the deep stuff. I went from being firmly in my element to completely out of control in a second.

"Yes, I guess," I barely mumbled.

Richard took to a deep breath, searching for the right words. Remember, he told the truth, no matter the situation.

"Okay, you've set yourself up, Nick," he said. "And now I'm going to let you knock yourself down. Please read the next paragraph."

Sh*t, holy sh*t. What was happening? And what did he mean by "let you knock yourself down"? My chest tightened, my ears burned, my cheeks turned red, and I did as exactly as he instructed next.

I read.

"People knew God perfectly well, but when they didn't treat him like God, refusing to worship him, they trivialized themselves into silliness and confusion" (Romans 1:21 MSG).

A stream of tears appeared, and my breath disappeared. I scrunched up my lips in some attempt to keep the tears from coming as I continued.

"So that there was neither sense nor direction left in their lives. They pretended to know it all but were illiterate regarding life" (Romans 1:22 MSG).

Now I was full-out ugly crying, and I didn't even care. My chest was openly heaving and searching for oxygen.

"They traded the glory of God who holds the whole world in his hands for cheap figurines you can buy at any roadside stand" (Romans 1:23 MSG).

I was broken. For the first time in my life, "they" was not someone else; it was me. I missed the only thing that mattered: to acknowledge my creator. I had traded the glory of God for something I could buy at 7-Eleven in the discount bin. And it had left me anything but thriving. Realizing the truth in that moment, I sobbed. I heaved. My prideful walls began to break.

Was that day easy for me? No! But Richard Hoffman cared enough about me to not let me walk out of that meeting without a hard dose of reality. Not because he wanted to hurt me, but because he cared enough about me to want me to thrive. I firmly believe every Good Entrepreneur needs a Richard Hoffman in their life. Someone who will call them out on their crap. Someone who will tell them the truth in any circumstance. Someone who cares enough about them to want to see them thrive no matter the cost.

Whether you find yourself in a season of burnout, struggle, or confusion—or if you've yet to get there just yet—I want you to stop and ask yourself, Who is my Richard Hoffman? Who will be honest with me? Who will help me thrive?

A MORAL INVENTORY

Richard Rohr likes to say that our ego needs separateness[105] and a lack of humility to thrive.[106] And boy, did I have an ego. I did not think I needed anybody's help. I did not believe that I needed to learn. I was my own god, searching for a ladder that I could ascend to heaven under my own power. That meeting changed my life, shattering my identity into a thousand pieces.

But Richard Hoffman wasn't done with me yet. Now, he would help me rebuild.

We walked through a process of creating a moral inventory. It's a process where you take into account relationships that haven't worked out the way you thought they would in your life. It's like being at a restaurant when someone you haven't seen in a while walks in. What do you do? Well, if it's someone who left you hurt or wounded (or you left them in a similar state), you immediately wish you were anywhere but sitting in that restaurant. That person would end up on your moral inventory list.

I created four columns on a sheet of paper. In the first column, I wrote down the names of those people with whom a relationship had left me hurt, wounded, scarred, or shamed.

In the column next to their name, I wrote down my expectations of that relationship. What had I hoped it would be? For example, if the name I had written down was from a romantic relationship, I would write down that my expectation would have been a safe, trustworthy, and faithful relationship.

In the third column, I wrote down the emotions that I felt when I realized the expectations weren't going to be met. So, for example, if my business partner stole from me, I would write down that I felt anger, sadness, or disgust.

In the final column, I wrote down the actions I took in response to the brokenness in the relationship. So, you might write down that you cut them off, threw their clothes out in the street, or told everyone about what a scumbag they were.

Now of course, the point of this exercise isn't really about the names on your list. It's designed to help you reflect, heal, and ultimately thrive.

Of course, I didn't get that at first. For my list, I picked five people who had objectively done bad things to me—people who I felt had screwed me over, breaking my trust in them. Even in this game, I wanted to win. I tried to manipulate it. I wanted to come out ahead. I wanted to look better than those who'd wronged me.

But that wasn't the point. And as I recounted their actions, I realized a pattern, not in their lives but in my own. Over and over again, my actions were to cut those people off. To rid them from my life and make them feel terrible on the way out. Their actions confirmed my deep-rooted belief that, ultimately, I couldn't truly trust anyone but myself. My responses were born out of that place.

Looking at this inventory on paper, I had to confront the fact that almost everybody on my list was there because of where I'd placed them on the chessboard of my life. In my mind, I was the king, and they were the pawns. And as a pawn is designed to do, their role was to protect the king and advance his desires. When someone didn't do that, I was angry. If they didn't like the spot I had put them in on my chessboard, I felt as though they were defying me. When they did that, I would cut off the relationship. Just like that, they'd be dead to me.

Even though all five people on my list had done horrible things to me, I had to acknowledge my own responsibility in those relationships if I wanted to be able to thrive going forward. I had to acknowledge that I didn't have the right over any other human being to manipulate them for my benefit. There was no cosmic chessboard in which everybody was playing. I didn't need to win to prove my worth. My *biography* was not my *identity*.

That truth broke me because I had held so close to my identity that I was a victim because of my father's conviction. I believed that my trauma was the result of the choices and actions of others alone. My identity revolved around picking myself up by my own bootstraps, dusting myself off, and overcoming what had happened to me. I'd become powerful. I'd been named the entrepreneur of the year! But as I looked at that piece of paper, none of that held weight. If I wanted to thrive going forward, I had to acknowledge my own brokenness.

POURING INTO OTHERS

Richard Hoffman has since passed away, but a few weeks prior to his death, his friend Jim Beckett hosted a dinner for about 20 of his friends. Around that large table as we ate, Jim spoke up and asked us to share what Richard meant to us. Richard, at the head of the table, was half of the physical man that he used to be, but his soul was alive and thriving.

The first man spoke. "Richard, when I was going through my divorce, you were my first call. You took my call late at night and agreed to meet with me every Monday at 10 a.m. for the last four years. You have been the friend I needed and a rock that I was able to rest on."

The next man went. "Richard, when I was about to lose my professional license because of the conviction of a felony, I wanted to end my life, but instead, I called you. You took my call, and you agreed to meet with me regularly at 3 p.m. on Thursdays. We've met for the last decade, and I am thankful for you because next week I am going to get my professional license back. I was on the verge of suicide a decade ago, and now I am being healed and restored."

Man after man told similar stories. We laughed, we cried, and we indulged in the moment for this man who had dedicated his life to helping us all thrive.

Toward the end of the table, a friend of Richard's spoke. "Richard, I'm going to tell my story, but first, I have a question for you. Bob said that he met with you at 10 a.m. on Monday, and Sam said he met with you at 12 p.m. on Wednesday, and John said he met with you at 3 p.m. on Thursday. And that story was repeated around this table multiple times. My question for you is: When did you ever work?"

Richard was a very successful business executive. In fact, he had just sold the business that he and his wife started. He was no slouch, and I can tell you that he most definitely had a full schedule.

He thought deeply and spoke quietly. "When I threw my life into chaos two decades ago, I began the process of realizing what was important in life, and at some point, I realized that my business was going to take second place to me pouring into other people who needed a friend when no other friend existed. It is really quite simple. Seeing people removing the cataracts from their eyes and moving into truth is the best feeling there is in the world. So why would I ever put anything in front of this opportunity?"

Witnessing the scene at this dinner shook me to my core. I drove away thinking about Richard, his legacy, and the lives he had changed. I wondered if anyone would say the same about me.

I believe it should be one of our goals as Good Entrepreneurs to not just find the Richard Hoffman in our lives but to *be* the Richard Hoffman in the lives of others. Part of thriving is seeking to help others thrive along the way. That's what Richard did for each of those men around the dinner table that night. He poured his life into us. And it would be a disservice to his legacy if I didn't seek to do the same for others.

YOU'RE GOING TO BE OKAY

Richard helped me deconstruct my life to its core elements, and now that I was conscious, I needed to *reconstruc*t myself with a new perspective. So, I found myself in a new position to learn and signed up for the Townsend Leadership Program.

The Townsend Leadership Program (TLP) was created by Dr. John Townsend and has helped a great number of participants over the years. In TLP, a group of 10 participants and a director spend a year at a time together, meeting once a month for a full day of programming. This time is spent working on our businesses and ourselves, learning from the process and each other.

About halfway through the 12-month TLP program, there is a day designated as the Affirmation and Challenge Day. On this day, the other participants in the group write down and share their observations about your journey, including both an affirmation and a challenge.

On this day in my group, I was second to last to go. I got to witness several other individuals ingest the truth that was being spoken into them. Even though I was watching closely and trying to prepare to receive my affirmation and challenges from the group, I was woefully unprepared to hear what they had to say.

If "I see you" from my wife was the amuse-bouche, then this process was the appetizer, salad, soup, entrée, and dessert with wine pairings from the hills of France. One by one, each participant read their affirmations and challenges to me, their words forever ensconced in my mind.

At the end of the readings, my director, Nancy, asked me how I felt. Through tears, I uttered the only words that I could possibly say:

"I feel like I am going to be okay."

My biggest fear had always been that I would never be able to do enough to provide for myself and my family. I have wondered if I was going to be okay from the moment my world was turned upside down at the loss of my father. Over two decades later, I finally had an answer to my eternal question. I was going to be okay, and you are too.

If you have the courage to pry open your emotional vault and take a peek inside.

If you have the willingness to ask for and accept help.

If you have the vulnerability to allow yourself to truly be seen.

You're going to be okay. In fact, you're going to be more than okay!

You're going to be able to thrive.

The reality is that there are myriad easier ways to make money than starting a business from scratch. So, if it's just money you're after, I don't recommend this path. But if it's influence you're after—if it's shaping the world you live in—there's truly no more rewarding path than the way of the Good Entrepreneur.

I am the son of a convicted felon, one who spent nearly two decades in prison. I went from being a statistic to finding quite a bit of success. I can tell you without a shadow of doubt that the difference between flying on a private plane and going to prison is just a few important decisions. And I can tell you that if you don't get clear on your purpose and your values, if you don't find some people who really love you and show up for you and tell you the truth, if you don't find a way to truly thrive, it won't matter all that much which place you land.

Private plane or prison cell—both can feel lonely and isolating.

But now that I know this, it's a superpower to me. Now it doesn't matter what kind of challenges I face in my life or what kind of outcomes I get—even if I don't get the outcomes I want. Because I have the things that I know will help me to thrive, not just as an entrepreneur but as a human being. I know my values. I have a vision. I'm surrounded by people who tell me the truth. I don't think of myself as a god anymore. And at the end of the day, I know I'm only as good as the legacy I leave behind.

My hope is that by the time you're done reading this book, you'll have all of that too.

END-OF-CHAPTER HOMEWORK
WHISPER

Take out your journal, write down the following questions, and answer them after some time of reflection:

- What whisper do you need to hear?
- What truth do you need to be told to set you free to thrive?
- If our real ability to thrive isn't about our net worth but about our true worth, what are you investing in to make yourself wealthy?
- If you have the courage to pry open your emotional vault and take a peek inside, what would you see?
- If you have the willingness to ask for and accept help, who would you ask? What would they say?
- If you have the vulnerability to allow yourself to truly be seen, what would people see?

Next, review the following eight basic emotions and their gifts and senses.

EIGHT BASIC EMOTIONS...		THEIR GIFTS	
ANGER	RESENTMENT IRRITATION FRUSTRATION	ASSERTIVENESS STRENGTH ENERGY	ALL OVER BODY Power Energy
FEAR	APPREHENSIVE OVERWHELMED THREATENED	PRESERVATION WISDOM PROTECTION	ALL OVER BODY UPPER CHEST Suffocation
PAIN	HURT PITY SAD LONELY	HEALING GROWTH AWARENESS	LOWER CHEST AND HEART Hurting
JOY	HAPPY ELATED HOPEFUL	ABUNDANCE HAPPINESS GRATITUDE	ALL OVER BODY Lightness
PASSION	ENTHUSIASM DESIRE ZEST	APPETITE ENERGY EXCITEMENT	ALL OVER BODY Energized Recharged Spontaneous
LOVE	AFFECTION TENDERNESS COMPASSION WARMTH	CONNECTION LIFE SPIRITUALITY	HEART Swelling Warmth
SHAME	EMBARRASSED HUMBLE	HUMILITY CONTAINMENT HUMANITY	FACE, NECK AND/OR UPPPER CHEST Warm Hot Red
GUILT	REGRETFUL CONTRITE REMORSEFUL	VALUES AMENDS CONTAINMENT	GUT Gnawing sensation

©Pia Mellody

Which one stands out as one that you know really well?
How does that manifest itself in your life?
Are there any others that you can relate to?
The next time you feel triggered, reflect back on this chart to unpack the emotion you are feeling.

PRINCIPLE TWELVE

LEAVE A POWERFUL PERSONAL LEGACY

LEAVE A LEGACY

One of the questions I think every Good Entrepreneur asks themselves at some point (or more likely, many points) in the journey is this:

What's next?

Not necessarily what's next for their business, or what's next for their product, or what's next for their team, or even what's next for themselves as a leader. No, when a Good Entrepreneur looks ahead and considers what's next, they're considering the road they've walked so far and the places they still want to go. The meaning they still want to make in this world. The impact they still feel called to have on other people.

The legacy they want to leave.

Isn't that what we're all trying to do? To leave this world and the people we encounter in it just a little better than we found them? To make a difference in this world that's bigger than the work we've done, or the products we've created, or the things we've accomplished?

Ultimately, that's what every Good Entrepreneur seeks to do: leave a legacy.

VULNERABILITY

I had the opportunity to speak at the David Gilbert Leadership Conference held for freshman leaders at Texas A&M. The program is named after David Gilbert, who passed away while attending Texas A&M. He was a leader whose legacy lives on today through these student leaders in this program that has been given his name. The program challenges those participants to live with a standard that goes beyond themselves, focusing on selfless leadership as their goal. It is a beautiful organization, and I was honored to be invited to share my story with them.

The topic of my presentation was supposed be my experience as an entrepreneur and the things I'd learned about balancing my personal and professional needs. I would be given 10 minutes to share, and then the freshmen would have five minutes to ask questions. At the conclusion, the students would move to another table to hear from a different executive.

I've given hundreds of speeches along the way, but may I make a confession here? I still have a bit of impostor syndrome. I'm always afraid that the audience will hear the words coming out of my mouth and quickly realize that deep down, I am really making it up as I go. To combat this fear, I work hard to understand my audience. I try to tailor my speeches directly to them, crafting a story that I think they'll like while also painting a flattering picture of who I am and what I've done.

In planning for this particular event, I had created a carefully crafted script designed to make the most of the 10 minutes I had been given and, of course, make the audience love me (hopefully!). But that day when I opened my mouth to speak, something different happened. I felt compelled to throw out the perfectly polished script and get real with these students instead. To be me, instead of the version of me I wanted to present. So, on impulse, I threw out my script and went with my heart, choosing to answer the call of vulnerability.

Vulnerability creates an interesting juxtaposition. In you, it is courageous and daring, but in me, it's weakness. It's one of the first things I look for in you, but it's the last thing I'm willing to show you in myself. We want to receive it, but we don't want to give it. This juxtaposition creates a tension, however, because vulnerability is key in relationships. If we want to be successful in relating to other people, we need vulnerability to be a cornerstone of not just how they relate to us but of how we relate to them.

And if we want to leave a legacy that's authentic to who we are as Good Entrepreneurs, we have to be willing to be vulnerable.

Remember RISE's first core value? Love. Even now, after several years and hundreds of conversations on this very topic, it still feels a little weird to say that, but like all truth, it becomes truer over time. If we could lead with love, we'd be leaving the legacy that we wanted for ourselves and our company in our wake.

Along the way, I discovered that part of leading with love means being vulnerable with the people around you. Because of that, I have tried to be more overtly vulnerable whenever the opportunity arises. I'm honest about the things in my life that have caused embarrassment or even threatened to push me into an isolating cycle of shame. I used to keep my fears packed deep down inside of myself, hoping that with enough time they would just go away. That never worked. They always came back like a boomerang, whacking me upside my head at the most inopportune times. Instead, I found freedom in vulnerability.

And there, speaking at the leadership conference at Texas A&M, I chose vulnerability again. It was the first time that I had publicly shared how my dad was a felon. How that led to my abandonment issues. How I wasn't nearly as confident as I led others to believe. How I wanted to be in charge so that people had to listen to me or lose their job. How, even after two decades of evidence to the contrary, I too often acted as if Angela and I were on different teams and she couldn't be trusted. How I was constantly scheming in my relationships with others to see how they could help my ascent and discarding them when I didn't need them anymore. How my house or my car or my bank account were props that I used to convey my worth. These were ugly, and they were true.

They were the truths that I'd hidden for decades. That which I tried to cover up with my ever-growing list of accomplishments. The side of me that didn't fit into the carefully crafted speech I had planned to give that day. Now those things were tumbling out of my mouth with a raw and unexpected vulnerability.

I didn't plan on being so vulnerable to this group, but when I opened my mouth, I spoke truth. I chose love. Because ultimately, that's how I want to be remembered. Vulnerability is part of the legacy I want to leave.

When I finished speaking, I was overwhelmed by the response.

These students were given an authentic, embarrassing, and honest glimpse at my first several decades on this Earth. I braced, waiting for their shock and condemnation.

But it never came.

Instead, they responded with respect and honor to my story and confirmed that part of that my legacy is in my vulnerability.

And I think that's true of every Good Entrepreneur. The more real we are with ourselves and others, the more authentic our legacy will be.

As writer Anne Lamott says in her book *Bird by Bird*, "If something inside of you is real, we will probably find it interesting, and it will probably be universal. So, you must risk placing real emotion at the center of your work. Write straight into the emotional center of things. Write toward vulnerability. Risk being unliked. Tell the truth as you understand it. If you're a writer, you have a moral obligation to do this. And it is a revolutionary act—truth is always subversive."[107]

I believe this is true in all of our work. Anyone can leave a legacy, but the Good Entrepreneur leaves a legacy that is vulnerable and real.

THE STRENGTH OF A FRIEND

One of the most important things to remember as a Good Entrepreneur is that our legacy isn't just marked by what we do or how we live; it's marked by the people who go with us. If the old adage *You're known by the company you keep* is true, then surrounding yourself with the right people is key to your present, your future, and your legacy.

My friend Jeremy called me a few years ago to ask me to drive with him from Cabo San Lucas, Mexico, to San Diego—the entire Baja Peninsula. Angela and I and our kids had spent most of the summer in Montana and Alaska and were about to fly back to Dallas from Anchorage when I saw his text. I immediately wanted to go, and Angela was quick to adjust her calendar to allow me to do the four-day trip.

On one of the mornings of this trip, I was writing in my journal when Jeremy asked me how things were going with my dad. I looked up and tears began to form in my eyes. There is no better sign that truth is about to come spilling out than when you feel the tears start to well up.

"You know, Jeremy, I am just really sad," I told him honestly. "I have had three chapters with my dad: pre-prison, prison, and post-prison. I grieved, as best I could, the prison chapter while he was in prison. And recently, I've had to grieve the post-prison period. I had so many built up expectations that just fell flat. But this summer, I had the realization that our pre-prison period—those ages from zero to 16—wasn't all that great either."

Most of my memories from of my father were enveloped in chaos. He physically assaulted coaches, referees, and people who stole his spaces in parking lots. And when he wasn't doing that, he was just yelling. Yelling at us mostly, while also asking us to lie to process servers at our front door. As I said—chaos.

The reality of this was only hitting me now as an adult, and it had been difficult to process. Jeremy's simple question opened the flood gates for me.

"I'm now realizing that the best of times with my dad are most likely behind me, and even the best of times were pretty sh*tty times. I'm just realizing that one more part of my story I thought was true was fiction."

It felt good to have someone to confess this to. There's something powerful about having a mensch sit in silence with you as you process a difficult reality. That day, Jeremy did that for me. He listened empathetically, giving me grace in his silence.

"I'm just realizing that everything I've been trying to build and communicate for the better part of my life was to prove he wasn't a reflection on me," I confessed. "On top of that, I've felt like a poser—like there was this special club for all the kids who had fathers. The kids in this club got lessons on how to tie a tie, change a tire, or ask someone out on a date. I wasn't given a key to this club and the accompanying insight into life to make sure things turned out okay for them. I had to figure out how to survive on my own." In that moment I was sad and mad and ashamed all at the same time.

I paused. "I know I've never really told you any of this stuff, but I think it's because I never fully understood it until right now."

Jeremy gave me the space to lean into my emotions that day. It's a skill I've had to work at, but it's work I know is worth it. And like most things in life, it's work that's better done with the strength of a friend by your side.

When I arrived home from that trip, Angela could tell something was wrong. I started to tell her that all was okay, but then I stopped. I had a choice: isolate from my feelings and from her or lean into my emotions and tell the truth.

"I'm just really sad," I confessed finally. "I'm no longer in charge of my business, people who used to ask for my opinion are silent, and I don't know what I am going to do next. I don't know who I am or what I'm working toward anymore. When your identity is your business and then you sell that business, there is no worse deal in the world."

Angela is one of the kindest people I know. But one of the things that makes her kindness so strong is that it's supported by her backbone of steel. When she was in residency, I remember a night she called to say the local news was in the hospital doing a story in which she might be featured. I eagerly turned on the television for the 10 p.m. news and waited to see my wife, the TV star, on television. About halfway through the news cycle, her hospital was featured with several nurses and doctors, but Angela was nowhere to be seen.

I picked up the phone to let her know that she didn't make the cut. When she answered, she was filled with excitement.

"How cool was that? I was on TV tonight!"

Dumbfounded, I told her I didn't see her and quickly pulled up the recorded session to look again. Sure enough, in the middle of the ER, there she was. Encased in bright lights, working on a patient, and surrounded by a supporting crew, Angela was barking orders for her patient. I did a double take and realized that this badass doctor was my wife. I had never seen her in her element, and I had a mix of elation and confusion trying to figure out who this woman was. Her backbone of steel was saving that patient's life.

And now, more than a decade later, that same woman showed up across the dining room table from me.

"What if this is just part of the process?" she asked. "A reminder that your biography isn't your identity. I would encourage you to get this into your journal so that you can remember that this is a process, not a means to an end."

We spoke for less than five minutes, but her truth carried so much swagger that it felt like a full day of counseling.

I'm more than my titles.

I'm more than my achievements.

I need to get out of survival mode.

I need to stop seeing everything in life as a means to the next end.

I need to trust the process.

I went to our bedroom and closed my eyes to meditate. When I did, an image came into my mind of Eustace Scrubb, a character from C. S. Lewis's book *The Voyage of the Dawn Treader*.[108]

Eustace was more of a pest than he was a help as a young boy, always finding a way to wander off to avoid having to do any work. In one such instance, he found a cave with an old dragon breathing its last breaths outside of it. There, he watched as the dragon died. After it began to rain, Eustace sought shelter inside the dragon's cave where he found an immense treasure that included a gold bracelet. He put on the bracelet, shoving it partway up his arm because it was too large for his size. He eventually fell asleep, but when he woke up, he had a bizarre feeling.

He found himself changed into a dragon.

And for a while, he enjoyed it. Eustace had a fine time being a dragon, but eventually, he realized that he was not created for it. His identity was in being Eustace, not a dragon.

Eager to rid himself of his skin, he was taken to a pool by a lion. Scratching and clawing himself, Eustace desperately tried to shed his scales like a snakeskin. After several times through this ordeal, he began to fear that he would never be rid of the scales. That's when a lion's voice told him, "You will have to let me undress you."

The lion tore the skin from Eustace, picked him up, and dropped him into the pool. As Eustace washed, he realized he had turned back into a boy. He returned to the camp and told his cousin Edmund what had happened to him. Edmund revealed that the lion must have been their wise friend and leader, Aslan.

That day, this childhood story reminded me of myself. I thought about the skin that I had shed and how I didn't have the power to do it myself. I thought back to Richard and how he had showed me that I was powerless against my pride and that because of pride my life had become unmanageable. Believing that there is a power greater than me was simultaneously the hardest and most comforting decision I had ever made. I needed to be rescued from the costume I had made for myself.

If you want to shed your skin and leave a legacy that shows your true self, you can't do it alone.

You have to rely on the strength of mensches and a higher power.

A NEW LEGACY

The lie so many of us are tempted to believe is that our legacy lies in our work. The awards we win, the titles we hold, the achievements we make, the money we earn—all that and more seems to add up to a pretty lofty legacy. And although this may be true for most people, it shouldn't be the case for us. As Good Entrepreneurs, our lives are about so much more than our work. Our work is about so much more than ourselves. And because of that, our legacies should be tied to the meaning we find, the difference we make, and the affect we have on others for good.

The trouble is the world wants to tell us something different. And so, as Good Entrepreneurs, we must work to tune out the wrong message and instead tune into our purpose and the kind of legacy we want to leave.

In November of 2017, my friend Don invited me to Carmel, California, to spend some time connecting with a few other men. I was ecstatic to be invited. The acquisition of RISE had happened a few months earlier, and the craziness of the transaction was now behind me. I was starting to sleep better, drink less, and work on being more intentional in my relationships. I was trying to build a new legacy for myself—one not necessarily attached to my work.

I landed in Carmel to find it a bit chilly and overcast—typical for a November day in Northern California. The airport was small, and within a few steps, I exited to my waiting car. Traffic was thick as we made our way past the downtown area and out past Point Lobos State Natural Reserve to the southern side of the city. In the instructions from Don's assistant, there was an address to head to and, strangely, also GPS coordinates. After driving by the location several times, I knew why: this house wasn't meant to be found.

A wall that framed a dirt parking area with just enough room for a few cars was the welcome mat to our home for the weekend. The waves could be heard crashing on the other side of the wall, and the unmistakable smell of saltwater mist hung in the air. A wooden door signaled the entrance to this house and the beginning of several new and deep friendships.

I knocked, but no one answered. The driver had left, and I was alone with my bag. I knocked again, and still, no one answered. So, I tried the door handle. And as the door gave way, I saw the slightest hint of the ocean just off to the left, down below a steep and treacherous drop-off. An intentionally natural landscape pointed to a path, and there I saw the house about 75 yards away. I entered what I believed to be the front door and found myself in the middle of a round room with a view to the Pacific Ocean.

"Hello," I muttered half-heartedly.

No answer.

I noticed a couple of other sets of luggage at my feet, so I dropped my backpack and walked down the stairs. A stately fireplace complete with soot up its plaster facade stood in front of two deep couches that sat facing each other. Beyond that was a table that looked to seat 12. As I was taking in the room, a man appeared out of nowhere.

"Welcome. Can I get you something to drink?" he asked.

With a drink in hand, I went out to the patio where I found Don seated with a few unfamiliar faces.

"Nick!" Don roared. "Welcome to the James house! Let me introduce you to the guys."

I shook hands and said hello to two or three guys, and we took a quick tour of the estate before settling in.

That night at dinner, I sat next to a man named Jason. If you believe Google, Jason is best known for being the creator of "Kony 2012," a short documentary that went viral on YouTube and shed light on the crimes of Joseph Kony in Uganda. The fallout from that viral video came when Jason ended up walking naked on the streets of San Diego at the height of a nervous breakdown.[109] However, there's so much more to him than the caricature painted through a Google search. That is nothing like the Jason I know. In my experience, Jason is one of the most thoughtful human beings in the world. He is a delightful mix of empathy and activism. He's the kind of person who will leave you changed. That, to me, is part of his legacy.

That night at dinner, Jason shared his story with us. It was beautiful, vulnerable, and honest. And I don't know that I have ever witnessed someone become so vulnerable so quickly. The tone of our time was set by Jason, and I am thankful for his courage.

I shared next, trying to follow Jason's lead and to open with honesty. As I spoke, I found my vulnerability embraced by these men. It put me at ease in their presence even though we had just met. Don had done what he does so well; he thoughtfully and intentionally invited a group of people together to learn from each other and challenge one another in life.

We bonded quickly as a group, so much so that by the very next night we were planning our next gathering together. The consensus was Israel. One of the guys, Chris, had led some tours there, and he was willing to lead this motley crew.

At some point, someone turned to me and asked, "How much would it be for all of us to fly private to Israel?"

This is the kind of question I had learned to answer almost as quickly as I could recite my name. Doing calculations like this became second nature because of my work at RISE. When asked, my brain snapped to attention. I made the calculations, added 20% just to be safe, and proudly announced the amount. And although I won't give you the exact number, I'll tell you this: that one round-trip flight with 20 people would be significantly more than the cost of my first house and only slightly less than my second.

From the far end of the table, one of them responded, "We know that is retail, but what kind of a deal can you get us?"

Now I felt important to the group. And suddenly, I found myself tempted to give in to the voice that told me my value amounted to my title. What unique information did I possess that they wanted? And how could I use this information to impress them?

Only now I didn't have a title.

"Well, if I still had direct access to planes, I might've been able to get a better deal," I informed them. "But it is what it is now."

I could see the disappointment rise among some of their faces as they realized they wouldn't be riding into the Holy Land on a discounted private plane. And then, a man who has since become a dear friend commented, "Well, if we'd known that you weren't going to have access to private planes, we may not have invited you to this group."

He was obviously joking, but it felt like whatever importance I had built up had suddenly left the dining room. I was triggered.

Within one second, my ears started to warm, my cheeks began to flush, and my chest tightened. What was that familiar feeling? Shame. Shame that I couldn't give these people what they wanted. Shame that I no longer had access to the thing that had given me worth. Shame that I had no title to lean on in this moment.

Within two seconds, I knew why I felt this shame. My identity as a founder and CEO had been sold away, and now I was standing naked in front of these people I desperately wanted to impress. I thought I had nothing of worth to show them.

And within three seconds, I felt it pass.

The old Nick would have felt the same physical response to the comment but not have been aware of it. The old Nick would have felt the shame but not understood it. The old Nick would have been threatened by this unintentional assault on his kingdom. The old Nick would have gone into survival mode, quickly turning to anger as a form of protecting his worth, tossing out some turn of phrase that would have had the whole table laughing at my wittiness while knowing it was designed to simultaneously embarrass and harm the speaker.

But the new Nick knew better. Because this version of myself knew the truth: That wasn't my worth, so it didn't matter what I could or couldn't offer to them.

I was building a new legacy, one that had little to do with private planes. And knowing the value of that is what kept me grounded that day.

IN THE ZONE

When you are in the zone, everything slows down. Your heart rate slows, your eyes become clear, and your mind is uninterrupted. The zone feels like a version of heaven on Earth to a baseball player, and once you have tasted it, nothing else will satiate your appetite.

Growing up, Tony Gwynn was one of my favorite baseball players., Gwynn never struck out more than 40 times a year and He had eight seasons (including six consecutive ones) when he had fewer than 20 strikeouts. His game was precise.

That type of precision doesn't happen unless you're in the zone.

Back when I played, I remember stringing together two or three solid games. I got hits off good pitchers, threw runners out at second, and nailed the victory. I was in the zone, and I wanted to do whatever I had to do to stay there. I would eat the same breakfast, wear the same socks, and listen to the same song, all so that I could squeeze out every last drop of success that the baseball gods had decided to bestow on me. The zone was where you wanted to be, and you'd do just about whatever it took to stay in it.

My friend Miles Adcox is one of a few human beings I know who seems to live *in the zone*. He listens intently, asks questions intentionally, and has somehow figured out how to make you feel like you are the only human who matters when you're with him. If he's in the zone, he's going to bring you along with him.

I met Miles that weekend in Carmel. I didn't know him before this encounter, but I would be forever changed by our meeting. Miles runs a healing facility called Onsite about an hour outside of Nashville that has helped thousands of people on their life journeys.

The morning after our infamous group dinner in Carmel, Miles and I took a walk to an outcropping of rocks that jutted out into the sea. A path among the rocks crossed a small and tired bridge and took us to a slight uphill with a beautiful view of the Pacific Ocean. As we walked, Miles shared his story with me. I was struck by how he had turned his life into a catalyst for helping thousands of humans.

"Miles, would you help me process something?" I slowly ventured into unknown territory. "Last night at dinner …"

I went on to reveal my insecurity, those three seconds after a flippant comment that threatened to call forth the old Nick. Miles didn't say a word, but his body language gave me the confidence to know he was with me. I shared with him what I'd been feeling—the fears, the shame, and the struggle to stand strong in this new Nick working to leave a new legacy.

Miles helped me get in the zone that day. He helped me remember what was true—about myself, my worth, and my legacy. And I knew from my baseball days that once I found myself grounded in the zone, I wanted to do what I had to do to stay there.

Good Entrepreneurs know how to live in the zone.

Because in this place, they find a sense of purpose and a clarity of vision that roots them. It grounds them in the reality of what they want for their lives. It helps them see a clear path forward to leaving the kind of legacy they want.

A legacy based in meaning, in purpose, and in impact. A legacy that brings goodness to the world.

BEGIN AGAIN

After this experience, I knew that I had to begin the process of defining my purpose, vision, and values for this new season of my life. Only, I didn't know exactly where to start. Luckily, two close mensches, Austin Mann and Don, separately encouraged me to look at a program called Life Plan with the Paterson Center in Boulder, Colorado. These two successful men knew when something was worth doing, and so when they suggested it, I took the opportunity to explore more.

Angela and I had to wait the better part of year to find an opening on Pete Richardson's calendar, and when we flew up to see him in October, it was cold and gloomy outside.

We were instructed to meet Pete at a small breakfast restaurant at 8 a.m. We walked into the restaurant that was converted from an old house, the boards creaking under years of service, and told the hostess that we were meeting Pete there.

She smiled broadly and welcomed us warmly as if she knew Pete and wanted to greet us well. Pete saw us walking in and got up from the table to introduce himself in person. He is tall, with glasses, no hair, and a welcoming smile that penetrates your soul. I was a little taken back by the familiarity, given that we had just met, but as we ordered coffee and our food, the conversation was unforced and natural.

After breakfast we followed in our rental car to his house on a quiet street and were led downstairs to his converted basement. He had been facilitating life planning sessions for over a decade, so when it came time to remodel their basement, he created a space designed for the process we were about to enter into.

The room was warm from the fire roaring in the fireplace and cozy because of how it was set up. Two chairs faced a whiteboard that spanned the length of the room from floor to ceiling and a rocking chair faced the chairs and the rest of the room. Pete sat in the chair and began to describe the process we were about to go through. The first part of the three days was designed to capture our life stories, and the second part of the session would be to identify what the path would look like going forward. We had told Pete that we wanted a 20-year strategic plan for our lives, and he agreed that was a good idea.

I have never been shy of wanting to talk about myself, but talking about yourself for eight hours a day is exhausting. Pete graciously gave us a space to share and laugh and cry. In doing so, we forced ourselves to be seen, and he diligently documented our stories. The final product was a 10-foot by five-foot piece of paper that showed our lives chronologically in five categories: personal, family, vocation, church, and community.

We took some time to ingest the information that was in front of us. Seeing the evidence of your four decades on this Earth is eerily calming. It is all there: the high times, the low times, the poor decisions, the regrets, and the pride. For me, I felt like I was on river time just like my brother-in-law had described.

Then Pete grabbed a red marker and asked us to name the major turning points in our story. He said most people have one or two turning points, those times at which the trajectory of our lives had changed forever. I thought about his question, and I could name the time when my dad went to prison. So, Pete put a red line down the section from when I was in high school. He asked if there were any additional times, and I searched the paper looking over the sum of my days, passing decades worth of time, until I came to the moment in which I was forever changed during my time with Richard Hoffman.

Pete moved the eight feet or so down the paper and placed another red line during that time, just a few short years ago. On those days, I was transformed, and yet I had woken up those mornings not knowing that anything was going to happen of any consequence. It was if God had leaned down and touched me with his finger, like a modern-day version of *The Creation of Adam* by Michelangelo.

We continued the process, naming the seasons of my life, and I was struck by the middle of my life map. Of the 10 feet of paper, about a third of it consisted of about 18 months of my life, starting with my moving to Arkansas and finishing with me meeting Angela. In that time, I transformed from someone who hadn't had any reason to live on I-70 in Colorado (or so I thought) to someone driven beyond comprehension. *In that season, named "dead man walking" and "the preparation years," I was held and protected like I should have been by my earthly father, but instead of my biological dad, many other people came into my life and played a vital part in my growth.*

The final step on the storyline was when Pete asked us to take a red marker and, on a scale from one to 10, name the number that we were at during that particular season. It started as a five and stayed there through my childhood, then dropped to a one (one being the worst) at 16, slowly rose to a nine when I married Angela, but dropped back down to the four-to-six range all the way to the sale of RISE, and finally peaked on the night I recognized that there is a God and it is not me.

I realized that the whole time I had felt marginalized, seemingly walking my path all alone, I was actually being held afloat by a whole host of people who chose to love me in both small and large ways, in one conversation, and in a multiyear relationship.

Then, Pete helped me summarize this process into one sentence that has become my new purpose in life: to create experiences that lead to truth telling and life change for billionaires, prisoners, and everyone in between.

ANSWER THE CALL

A few weeks before Richard Hoffman died, I drove to his lake house for one last conversation. As I stepped onto the back deck, I was shocked to see how much weight he had lost since our last time together. However, I quickly found out that his body belied the strength in his mind.

He greeted me with a smile, and as I hugged him, I could feel his shoulder blade a little too well. Our eyes connected as we embraced, and tears welled up. This lion of man was a ghost of who he used to be, and he knew it. He chuckled a little as if to say, "Well, I guess we can't win them all."

We both settled into our seats, choosing to embrace the silence and feel the presence of each other, knowing it would be the last time. We watched kids running by the lake and the birds flying from tree to tree. Lynn brought us some water and let us continue our meditation.

After a while I opened my mouth and spoke, "Richard, you have been such a powerful force in my life. Thank you for having the courage to get in the well with me as I wrestled my demons; I am forever changed."

The tears began to flow rapidly as I wished this day would never end. I continued, "How can I ever thank you for the impact you have had on me?"

Richard looked off into the distance, smirked a little, and said words that would change my life, "Whatever I did for you, look for others to do the same. Don't be afraid to get into the mess of life; embrace it and sit with people in their worst days, and help them see and tell the truth that they know."

I looked him in the eye and said, "I will."

We embraced, and with that, I gave Richard one last deep look, trying to memorize the lines on his face to call on later, and walked off his porch.

MY NEW RISE

In a seemingly offhand comment years prior, Angela suggested that RISE might be "the thing before the thing." I scoffed at her suggestion—how would I ever top starting, growing, and selling an airline? That was clearly "the thing" that I would be known for.

Since that suggestion, Angela and I have implemented a system in our lives that we call "micro-retirement," where we spend two weeks a month generating revenue and two weeks of our time exploring aspects of our lives that we would otherwise have ignored because of a seeming lack of return on investment. This book is the first material that I have created from my micro retirement.

On the revenue-generating side, I have started and grown an executive coaching business, Nick Kennedy Coaching, where I do two main things. First, I lead groups of executives on a 12-month journey where we work on integrating the principles of *The Good Entrepreneur* into every aspect of our lives. We spend a full day together once a month for a year, plus we have a weekend retreat with spouses or significant others in Steamboat Springs, where we have a home. Second, I work with a select group of leaders one-on-one to help them as they build their businesses and legacies. We spend sacred time together working through the issues that ail us so that we can learn to thrive as Good Entrepreneurs.

Because Pete Richardson helped point me toward my purpose, I now live most of my days on river time, and the fulfillment I receive by walking alongside leaders is beyond my wildest imagination. I am living the life of a Good Entrepreneur.

LEGACY

So, the question is this: What is the legacy you want to leave?

Anyone can start a business, build a product, or make a mark in their industry. With a little hard work and the right doors to open, any entrepreneur can find success. Anyone can make their work their legacy.

But not everyone can be a Good Entrepreneur. Not everyone will choose to walk the path that leaves the kind of legacy that matters. The kind of mark that makes a difference. The kind of impact that amounts to so much more than money, or status, or ambition. Good Entrepreneurs know their legacies are about the kind of lives they lead, the way they love, and the people they influence for the better.

My charge to you is this: do not be too easily pleased. The world needs more Good Entrepreneurs. In fact, I think the world is calling for us to wake up and step out of the shadows, to set ourselves apart from the rest, and to make a mark that matters.

Will you answer the call?

Will you become the Good Entrepreneur?

ENDNOTES

1. "Number of Starbucks Worldwide 2021/2022: Facts, Statistics, and Trends," Finances Online, accessed September 6, 2021, https://financesonline.com/number-of-starbucks-worldwide/.

2. "Wendy Kopp," *Team* (blog), World Bank, accessed September 6, 2021, https://blogs.worldbank.org/team/wendy-kopp.

3. Jasmine Enberg, "Amazon Around the World," Insider Intelligence, November 13, 2018, https://www.emarketer.com/content/amazon-around-the-world.

4. Howard H. Stevenson and J. Carlos Jarillo, "A Paradigm of Entrepreneurship: Entrepreneurial Management," in *Entrepreneurship: Concepts, Theory and Perspective*, eds. Álvaro Cuervo, Domingo Ribeiro, and Salvador Roig (Berlin: Springer Science Business Media, 2007), 155–170.

5. Jeffrey K. McKee, Frank E. Poirier, and W. Scott McGraw, *Understanding Human Evolution* (London: Routledge, 2016), 23.

6. Ann Gibbons, "Food for Thought: Did the First Cooked Meals Help Fuel the Dramatic Evolutionary Expansion of the Human Brain?" *Science* 316, no. 5831 (2007): 1558–1560. For a general discussion see: Suzanne Collins, *Catching Fire* (New York: Scholastic Press, 2009).

7. "Tiny Ancient Shells—80,000 Years Old—Point to Earliest Fashion Trend," ScienceDaily, August 27, 2009. www.sciencedaily.com/releases/2009/08/090827101204.htm.

8. "80,000 year old shells point to earliest cultural trend," Cordis, European Commission, September 8, 2009. https://cordis.europa.eu/article/id/113680-80000-year-old-shells-point-to-earliest-cultural-trend/es.

9. Ian Tattersall, "Homo Sapiens: Meaning, Characteristics, & First Appearance," *Encyclopedia Britannica Online*, accessed June 28, 2021, www.britannica.com/topic/Homo-sapiens.

10. Nicholas R. Longrich, "Did Neanderthals Go to War with Our Ancestors?" BBC, November 2, 2020, https://www.bbc.com/future/article/20201102-did-neanderthals-go-to-war-with-our-ancestors.

11. "The Rise of Egyptian Civilization," Boundless, accessed, http://oer2go.org/mods/en-boundless/www.boundless.com/world-history/textbooks/boundless-world-history-i-ancient-civilizations-enlightenment-textbook/ancient-egypt-1/introduction-to-ancient-egypt-912/the-rise-of-egyptian-civilization-913-17525/index.html.

12. Roy MacLeod, ed., *The Library of Alexandria: Centre of Learning in the Ancient World*, (New York: IB Tauris, 2010), 61–78.

13. Thomas DeMichele, "Fibonacci Introduced the Modern Numeral System to Europe—Fact or Myth?" Fact/Myth, February 6, 2017, https://www.factmyth.com/factoids/fibonacci-introduced-the-modern-numeral-system-to-europe/.

14. Tabea Tietz, "Thomas Savery and the Invention of Steam Power," SciHi Blog, May 10, 2018, http://scihi.org/thomas-savery-invention-steam-power/.

15. Richard L. Hills, *Power from Steam: A History of the Stationary Steam Engine* (Cambridge: Cambridge University Press, 1989).

16. Luke Muehlhauser, "How Big a Deal Was the Industrial Revolution," accessed on, http://lukemuehlhauser.com/industrial-revolution/.

17. W. Michael Cox and Richard Alm, *Myths of Rich and Poor: Why We Are Better Off Than We Think* (New York: Basic Books, 1999); See also: G. Easterbrook, *The Progress Paradox* (New York: Random House, 2006).

18. Brink Lindsey, *The Age of Abundance: How Prosperity Transformed America's Politics and Culture* (London: Collins, 2007).

19. "The Next Chapter of the Generations Campaign," Patek Philippe, September 10, 2019, https://www.patek.com/en/company/news/generations-campaign.

20. C.S. Lewis. The Screwtape Letters, San Francisco: Harper, 1942, Harper edition 2001, pp. 154-155.

21. Roger Connors and Tom Smith, *The Wisdom of Oz: Using Personal Accountability to Succeed in Everything You Do* (New York: Portfolio, 2016).

22. Kathryn Orford, *Become Your #1 Fan: How to Silence Your Inner Critic and Live the Life of Your Dreams* (Queensland: Kathryn Orford, 2015).

23. John O'Donohue, "The Inner Landscape of Beauty," On Being (blog), August 31, 2017, https://onbeing.org/programs/john-odonohue-the-inner-landscape-of-beauty-aug2017/.

24. C. Suetonius Tranquillus, "Chapter 3," in *Suetonius: The Lives of the Twelve Caesars; An English Translation, Augmented with the Biographies of Contemporary Statesmen, Orators, Poets, and Other Associates*, eds. J. Eugene Reed and Alexander Thomson, (Philadelphia: Gebbie & Co., 1889), http://www.perseus.tufts.edu/hopper/text?doc=Perseus%3Atext%3A1999.02.0132%3Alife%3Daug.%3Achapter%3D29.

25. *The Little Mermaid*, directed by Ron Clements and John Musker (1989, Walt Disney Pictures), 83 mins.

26. Doree Lewak, "The College Dropout behind NYC's Most Exclusive Credit Card," *New York Post*, June 28, 2015, nypost.com/2014/07/05/the-22-year-old-dropout-who-created-nycs-most-exclusive-credit-card.

27. *Fyre Fraud*, directed by Jenner Furst (2019, Hulu), streamed, 96 mins.

28. John Carreyrou, *Bad Blood: Secrets and Lies in a Silicon Valley Startup* (New York: Vintage, 2020).

29. Ibid.

30. Dan Blystone, "The Story of Uber," Investopedia, January 10, 2021, www.investopedia.com/articles/personal-finance/111015/story-uber.asp.

31. Deborah Petersen, "Theranos CEO Elizabeth Holmes: 'Avoid Backup Plans,'" Inc., February 10, 2015, https://www.inc.com/deborah-petersen/elizabeth-holmes-avoid-backup-plans.html.

32. *Titanic*, directed by James Cameron (1995, Paramount Pictures), 195 mins.

33. Ibid.

34. Thomas J. Stanley and William D. Danko, *The Millionaire Next Door: The Surprising Secrets of America's Wealthy* (Lanham: Taylor Trade Publishing, 2010).

35. Plato, *The Republic of Plato*, translated by B. Jowett (London: Henry Frowde, 1888).

36. Ryan Holiday, *The Obstacle Is the Way: The Timeless Art of Turning Trials into Triumph* (New York: Portfolio, 2014).

37. Blake Morgan, "The Top 5 Industries Most Hated by Customers," *Forbes*, October 16, 2018, https://www.forbes.com/sites/blakemorgan/2018/10/16/top-5-most-hated-industries-by-customers/?sh=53670f0790b5.

38. Viktor E. Frankl, *Man's Search for Meaning* (Boston: Beacon Press, 2006).

39. Catherine Robson, "Investing in Times of Trouble: Don't Let a Crisis Go to Waste," *The Age*, July 29, 2016, https://www.theage.com.au/money/investing/investing-in-times-of-trouble-dont-let-a-crisis-go-to-waste-20160729-gqgxxx.html.

40. J. R. R. Tolkien, *The Hobbit* (Boston: Houghton Mifflin Harcourt, 2012).

41. "Helmuth von Moltke 1800–91," Oxford Reference, accessed September 6, 2021, https://www.oxfordreference.com/view/10.1093/acref/9780191826719.001.0001/q-oro-ed4-00007547.

42. Mike Berardino, "Mike Tyson Explains One of His Most Famous Quotes," *Sun-Sentinel*, November 9, 2012.

43. Dean Takahashi, "Intel CEO: Bad Companies Are Destroyed by Crises … Great Companies Are Improved by Them," Venture Beat, April 23, 2020, https://venturebeat.com/2020/04/23/intel-ceo-bad-companies-are-destroyed-by-crises-great-companies-are-improved-by-them/.

44. Juju Chang and Mary Claude Foster, "'Pharmaceutical Companies Must Take Responsibility,'" ABC News, August 6, 2008, https://abcnews.go.com/Health/story?id=5441082&page=1.

45. https://www.bloomberg.com/news/articles/2008-07-07/fresenius-agrees-to-buy-app-for-up-to-4-6-billion

46. Katie E. Martin, "The Earhart Brand," Flight Paths: Purdue University's Aerospace Pioneers (blog), Purdue, April 21, 2016, https://flightpaths.lib.purdue.edu/blog/2016/04/21/the-earhart-brand/.
47. Phil Knight, Shoe Dog: A Memoir by the Creator of Nike (New York: Scribner, 2016).
48. Max Roser, Esteban Ortiz-Ospina, and Hannah Ritchie, "Life Expectancy," Our World in Data, updated October 2019, https://ourworldindata.org/life-expectancy.
49. James Boswell, The Life of Samuel Johnson (New York: Penguin Classics, 2008).
50. Sam Roberts, "William Sokolin, Wine Seller Who Broke Famed Bottle, Dies at 85," New York Times, May 2, 2015, https://www.nytimes.com/2015/05/03/nyregion/william-sokolin-wine-seller-who-broke-famed-bottle-dies-at-85.html.
51. Ibid.
52. Donald P. Baker, "3 Who Stole Traffic Signs Sentenced to 15 Years," Washington Post, June 21, 1997, https://www.washingtonpost.com/archive/politics/1997/06/21/3-who-stole-traffic-signs-sentenced-to-15-years/14c0a68c-e8fd-42ba-881c-454f442a27f8/.
53. Ibid.
54. Chris Cwick, "The Pitcher Who Gave Up No. 756 to Barry Bonds Reflects 10 Years Later," Yahoo! Sports, August 7, 2017, https://sports.yahoo.com/pitcher-gave-no-756-barry-bonds-reflects-10-years-later-175522495.html.
55. Bacsik Fired for Racially Insensitive Tweet," ESPN, April 27, 2020, https://www.espn.com/dallas/mlb/news/story?id=5141002.
56. Monte Burke, Saban: The Making of a Coach (New York: Simon & Schuster, 2016).
57. Henry Cloud and John Townsend, Boundaries: When to Say Yes, How to Say No to Take Control of Your Life (Grand Rapids, MI: Zondervan, 1992).
58. "'You've Got to Find What You Love,' Jobs Says," Stanford News, June 14, 2005, https://news.stanford.edu/2005/06/14/jobs-061505/.
59. Bessel Van Der Kolk, The Body Keeps the Score: Brain, Mind, and Body in the Healing of Trauma (New York: Penguin, 2015).
60. "6 September (1955): Flannery O'Connor to Betty Hester," The American Reader, accessed September 7, 2021, https://theamericanreader.com/6-september-1955-flannery-oconnor/.
61. Leo Rostein, The Joys of Yiddish (New York: Pocket, 1991).
62. Adam Hayes, "Adam Smith and 'The Wealth of Nations,'" Investopedia, updated April 28, 2021, https://www.investopedia.com/updates/adam-smith-wealth-of-nations/.
63. Adam Smith, "An Inquiry into the Nature and Causes of the Wealth of Nations," accessed September 7, 2021, https://geolib.com/smith.adam/won1-02.html.
64. Jonathan Schlefer, "There Is No Invisible Hand," Harvard Business Review, April 10, 2012, https://hbr.org/2012/04/there-is-no-invisible-hand.
65. Christina Majaski, "Invisible Hand Definition," Investopedia, updated July 23, 2020, https://www.investopedia.com/terms/i/invisiblehand.asp.

66 Robert N. Bellah, *Habits of the Heart: Individualism and Commitment in American Life* (Berkeley: University of California Press, 2007).

67 Mark Buchanan, "Wealth Happens," *Harvard Business Review*, April 2002, https://hbr.org/2002/04/wealth-happens.

68 "Unwrapping the Gift of Connection," Prison Fellowship, accessed September 7, 2021, https://www.prisonfellowship.org/about/angel-tree/angel-tree-christmas/.

69 "Providing Coast-to-Coast Relief," Convoy of Hope, accessed September 7, 2021, https://www.convoyofhope.org.

70 "William Wilberforce," *Encyclopedia Britannica Online*, updated August 20, 2021, https://www.britannica.com/biography/William-Wilberforce.

71 Aleksandr Solzhenitsyn, *The Gulag Archipelago 1918–1956: An Experiment in Literary Investigation* (New York: Basic Books, 1997).

72 "Conscious Capitalism Exists to Elevate Humanity," Conscious Capitalism®, accessed September 7, 2021, https://www.consciouscapitalismchicago.org/Conscious-Capitalism.

73 A. H. Maslow, *A Theory of Human Motivation* (Eastford: Martino Fine Books, 2013).

74 Tony Schwartz, "Companies That Practice 'Conscious Capitalism' Perform 10x Better," *Harvard Business Review*, April 4, 2013, https://hbr.org/2013/04/companies-that-practice-conscious-capitalism-perform.

75 Simon Sinek, *Start with Why: How Great Leaders Inspire Everyone to Take Action* (New York: Portfolio, 2009).

76 "How Millennial Trophies Created a Generation of Workaholics," *Atlantic*, accessed September 7, 2021, https://www.theatlantic.com/sponsored/project-time-off/how-millennial-trophies-created-a-generation-of-workaholics/1260/.

77 Kristen Hadeed's personal website, https://www.kristenhadeed.com.

78 Kristen Hadeed, *Permission to Screw Up: How I Learned to Lead by Doing (Almost) Everything Wrong* (New York: Portfolio, 2017).

79 Brené Brown, "Listening to Shame," TED video on YouTube, March 16, 2012, https://www.youtube.com/watch?v=psN1DORYYV0.

80 Roman Krznaric, *The Good Ancestor: How to Think Long Term in a Short-Term World* (London: Virgin Digital, 2020).

81 Jonathan Hedger, "The Marketing Rule of 7, and Why It's Still Relevant in B2B," B2B Marketing, July 5, 2019, https://www.b2bmarketing.net/en/resources/blog/marketing-rule-7-and-why-its-still-relevant-b2b.

82 "Mission Statement," American Cancer Society online, January 12, 2017, https://www.cancer.org/about-us/who-we-are/mission-statements.html.

83 "Vision vs. Mission Statement," Sharp School, accessed November 5, 2021, http://p2cdn4static.sharpschool.com/UserFiles/Servers/Server_5439645/File/Board%20Meeting/Vision%20vs.%20Mission.pdf.

84 Daniel W. Rasmus, "Defining Your Company's Vision," Fast Company, February 28, 2012, https://www.fastcompany.com/1821021/defining-your-companys-vision.

85. "What is Nike's Mission?" Nike online, accessed November 5, 2021, https://www.nike.com/help/a/nikeinc-mission.
86. "Tesla's mission is to accelerate the world's transition to sustainable energy," Tesla online, accessed November 5, 2021, https://www.tesla.com/about.
87. "Our Mission: Spread ideas," TED online, accessed November 5, 2021, https://www.ted.com/about/our-organization.
88. About Amazon Staff, "Our mission: We aim to be Earth's most customer centric company," Amazon online, accessed November 5, 2021, https://www.aboutamazon.co.uk/uk-investment/our-mission.
89. "Vision vs. Mission Statement," Sharp School.
90. Gary Keller and Jay Papasan, *The One Thing: The Surprisingly Simple Truth about Extraordinary Results* (Austin: Bard Press, 2013).
91. Ben Horowitz, *The Hard Thing about Hard Things: Building a Business When There Are No Easy Answers* (New York: Harper Business, 2014).
92. "Enough with the Awards Shows Already," *Starting Line Writings* (blog), Starting Line, September 15, 2019, https://www.startingline.vc/blog/2019/9/15/enough-with-the-award-shows-already.
93. Horowitz, *The Hard Thing About Hard Things*.
94. Christopher Elliot, "It's Time for the Uber of Air Travel," *Washington Post*, July 30, 2015, https://www.washingtonpost.com/lifestyle/travel/its-time-for-the-uber-of-air-travel/2015/07/30/09c4c8c2-353a-11e5-8e66-07b4603ec92a_story.html.
95. Ben Horowitz, "Nobody Cares," Business Insider, updated October 8, 2011, https://www.businessinsider.com/nobody-cares-2012-3.
96. Andy Reinhardt, "Steve Jobs: 'There's Sanity Returning,'" Bloomberg, May 24, 1998, https://www.bloomberg.com/news/articles/1998-05-25/steve-jobs-theres-sanity-returning.
97. Tony Long, "Sept. 25, 1929: Doolittle Proves You Can Fly Blind," *Wired*, September 25, 2007, https://www.wired.com/2007/09/sept-25-1929-doolittle-proves-you-can-fly-blind/.
98. Kevin Freiberg and Jackie Freiberg, *Nuts!: Southwest Airlines' Crazy Recipe for Business and Personal Success* (New York: Currency, 1998).
99. Ibid.
100. Ray Dalio, *Principles: Life and Work* (New York: Simon & Schuster, 2017).
101. Ibid.
102. Amy Zipkin, "All You Can Fly, for a Monthly Subscription," *New York Times*, October 26, 2015, https://www.nytimes.com/2015/10/27/business/all-you-can-fly-for-a-monthly-subscription.html.
103. Danielle Abril et al., "EY Entrepreneur of the Year 2017," *D Magazine*, July-August 2017, https://www.dmagazine.com/publications/d-ceo/2017/july-august/ey-entrepreneur-of-the-year-2017/.

104 Scott McCartney, "The All-You-Can-Fly Experience," *Wall Street Journal*, updated June 15, 2016, https://www.wsj.com/articles/the-all-you-can-fly-experience-1466008481.

105 Richard Rohr, "Separateness Is Suffering," Center for Action and Contemplation, September 3, 2020, https://cac.org/separateness-is-suffering-2020-09-03/.

106 Richard Rohr, "John of the Cross, Part III: Humility," Center for Action and Contemplation, July 31, 2015, https://cac.org/john-cross-part-iii-humility-2015-07-31/.

107 Anne Lamott, *Bird by Bird: Some Instructions on Writing and Life* (New York: Anchor, 1995).

108 C. S. Lewis, *The Voyage of the Dawn Treader* (New York: HarperCollins, 1994).

109 Matt Williams, "Kony 2012 Campaigner Jason Russell: 'I Wasn't in Control of My Mind or Body,'" *Guardian*, October 8, 2012, https://www.theguardian.com/world/2012/oct/08/kony-2012-jason-russell-interview-nbc.

ACKNOWLEDGMENTS

Writing a book is harder than I thought and more rewarding than ever imagined. None of this would have happened if Christine Giella hadn't suggested I write a book and that I should reach out to Don Miller for help. I didn't know Don, but 72 hours later, Pierce Bush called to invite us to his wedding and said, "I have a friend named Don Miller that will be at the wedding, and the two of you should meet." Shortly after that, Don connected me with Ally Fallon, who told me that everyone should write a book because it is the best therapy you can get. She was correct and has been my friend, guide, and coach throughout this process. Thank you, Christine, Don, Pierce, and Ally; this book wouldn't exist without you.

I'm eternally grateful to my wife Angela, who was a wise guide for me and infinitely patient with my endless questions and thoughts as I wrote. Thank you for kindly correcting me, providing feedback, and encouraging me to set aside the necessary time to write this book. You have taught me how to love, how to be discerning, and how to be loyal. Home was a dream, one that I'd never seen until you came along.

To my children. I want to be known by you. I want the good, the bad, and the ugly of my life to be on display for you so that we can be connected. This book is part of my attempt to do that. I wrote nearly 140,000 words that were edited down to the 60,000 words found on these pages. The additional 80,000 words were not meant for general consumption, but they are full of very personal stories that you are welcome to at any time. Thank you for the joy you have brought me; I cannot wait to see what the future holds for us.

Writing a book about the story of your life is a surreal process that makes you grateful for the people that played a significant role in your life. I'm forever indebted to Richard Hoffman, Nancy Houston, Dr. John Townsend, Miles Adcox, and Pete Richardson, who walked alongside me in my journey of becoming self-aware, helping me face the ugly parts of my story, and finally guiding me in rebuilding with purpose.

Ally Fallon, Sara Shelton and the team at Find Your Voice, Julie Broad, Roy Rocha, Jaqueline Kyle, Melissa Sobey, Shane Vigeant, Nicole Larson, and the team at Book Launchers for their editorial help, keen insight, and ongoing support in bringing my stories to life. Tom Browning and Austin Mann read, edited and provided helpful feedback to the manuscript. Because of their efforts and encouragement, I was able to pass on a tangible token of my story to my family, where one didn't exist before.

To the employees, co-founders, investors, and members of RISE who helped build a company of purpose and allowed me to be their leader. Thank you for letting me serve, for being a part of our amazing company, and for showing up every day and helping our dream become a reality.

To all the entrepreneurs out there solving complex problems, building products or services, and creating cultures that invest in your stakeholders. I salute you, and I see you. When the going gets tough, know that I am in your balcony cheering for you, and when you get the win that seemed impossible, I will be celebrating with you. Honor those entrepreneurs that came before us by making sure to leave this world better than you found it.

LET'S KEEP THE CONVERSATION GOING!

Download worksheets and additional resources designed to strengthen your oganization and help you continue the conversation, thegoodentrepreneurbook.com

Order discounted bulk purchases of this book for your company, organization, or community at hello@sleepinggiantbooks.com

Book Nick Kennedy for speaking events or consultation contact hello@nickkennedycoaching.com

CONNECT WITH NICK KENNEDY

- WEBSITE: thegoodentrepreneurbook.com
- TWITTER: @nickkennedy_tw
- INSTAGRAM: @nickkennedy_ig
- LINKEDIN: linkedin.com/in/nickkennedycoaching

THANK YOU
FOR READING!

If you enjoyed THE GOOD ENTREPRENEUR, please leave a review on Goodreads or on the retailer site where you purchased this book and help me reach more readers like you, or recommend this book to someone who needs it! thegoodentrepreneurbook.com/contact

Made in the USA
Columbia, SC
19 February 2022